Financial Crises - A Selection of Readings

Edited by Stelios Markoulis

Published in London, United Kingdom

IntechOpen

Supporting open minds since 2005

Financial Crises - A Selection of Readings
http://dx.doi.org/10.5772/intechopen.80791
Edited by Stelios Markoulis

Contributors
Shanuka Senarath, Dogus Emin, Mouna Aloui, Hirokuni Iiboshi, Shin-Ichi Nishiyama, Ryo Hasumi, Tatsuyoshi Matsumae, Stelios Markoulis

First published in London, United Kingdom, 2021 by IntechOpen
IntechOpen is the global imprint of INTECHOPEN LIMITED, registered in England and Wales, registration number: 11086078, 5 Princes Gate Court, London, SW7 2QJ, United Kingdom
Printed in Croatia

British Library Cataloguing-in-Publication Data
A catalogue record for this book is available from the British Library

Additional hard and PDF copies can be obtained from orders@intechopen.com

Financial Crises - A Selection of Readings
Edited by Stelios Markoulis
p. cm.
Print ISBN 978-1-78923-857-0
Online ISBN 978-1-78923-858-7
eBook (PDF) ISBN 978-1-78985-339-1

For EU product safety concerns:
IN TECH d.o.o., Prolaz Marije Krucifikse Kozulić 3, 51000 Rijeka, Croatia, info@intechopen.com or visit our website at intechopen.com.

Meet the editor

Stelios Markoulis is an Associate Professor of Finance at the Cyprus Institute of Management and a member of the visiting teaching faculty at the University of Cyprus. He is also an Honorary Visiting Research Fellow at the City University Business School, London. He has also worked for several years in the financial services industry and in particular in the area of investment banking. His main research interests currently focus on bank distress and regulation, as well as the effects of exogenous shocks, such as terror attacks, on capital and foreign exchange markets. In the past he has also undertaken research regarding the determinants of stock returns and capital raising through the stock market. He has published over 20 papers in international peer-reviewed academic journals and has contributed chapters to several books.

Contents

Preface

This book is about financial crises and it is written at a time when the whole world is facing yet another crisis, a different one this time; one that is related to health, but which is also already affecting the global economy in quite a painful manner. Amidst the grief and pain caused by the Covid-19 pandemic, the world must also find ways to combat its economic consequences. So far, we have seen bold moves by several governments and central banks, which through the combined use of fiscal and monetary policy measures are trying to mitigate the economic effects of Covid-19. The first chapter of this book provides an initial overview of the effects of the pandemic on the global economy and in particular on the financial sector and banks and by doing so provides a "bridge" for the chapters that will follow and which address various aspects of the previous financial crisis (2007-2009).

There is no doubt that the Global Financial Crisis (GFC) of 2007-2009 is an important point of reference in the literature of economic and – in particular – financial crisis; inevitably, this book focuses on this crisis in several dimensions. One of the themes discussed extensively after the GFC was corporate governance and whether failures in this aspect were related and to what extent to the unfolding of the GFC. Chapter 2 addresses this issue by examining the relationship between stock volatility and outside directors and independent directors for a sample of French firms over the period 2006-2012. Results indicate that outside directors and audit size tend to increase the stock return volatility. Moreover, results also indicate that independent directors and ROA have a negative effect on the volatility of stock returns, thus contributing to stabilizing the behavior of the price of stocks.

The third chapter turns its attention to the sources of the Great Recession, and document the following three important findings: firstly, the "net-worth shock" of financial firms had gradually declined prior to a huge decrease of the net worth of non-financial firms; secondly, the net worth shock of non-financial firms accounted for a large proportion of the business cycle after the Great Recession; and finally, the Troubled Asset Relief Program (TARP) would have immediately worked to improve balance sheets of financial institutions. It is worth noting that the chapter also presents evidence that the aforementioned were further worsened by the collapse of the Lehman Brothers in September 2008.

Chapter 4 discusses the political and institutional dynamics behind the Global Financial Crisis. More specifically, the chapter focuses on asset securitization, which by reducing lending rates and transaction costs and enhancing liquidity in the market, has been described as the alchemy that "really works". Nonetheless, the chapter points out that this has been questioned in the context of the Global Financial Crisis by presenting a number of factors, which made the alchemy not work very well. More specifically, such factors are subprime lending, executive compensation, and de-regulation, among others, which the chapter discusses both from a political and institutional perspective.

The final chapter of the book presents an interesting case for Turkey and more specifically focuses on the effect of external factors on Turkish short-term interest rates and exchange rates. The analysis presents findings over both tranquil and politically stressed periods of time; the overall period examined is 2011-2018. The factors employed are the short-term interest rates of the USA and emerging markets risk premia and the chapter points out that even a little political development may cause serious volatility in the market.

The ideas presented in this book are hopefully fresh and stimulating; however, it should be noted that these are owed not only to the research carried out in this book, beyond that, but they have also often been "borrowed" from other exceptional researchers, as well as to discussions with a number of curious students. We would like to thank all of them. Moreover, I would also like to thank the IntechOpen publishing team, and in particular, Ms. Rozmari Marijan, Ms. Rebekah Pribetic, and Ms. Mia Vulovic for their patience and great support throughout this project.

Dr. Stelios Markoulis,
University of Cyprus/Cyprus International Institute of Management,
Cyprus

Section 1

Introduction

Chapter 1

Introductory Chapter: Financial Crises

Stelios N. Markoulis

1. Introduction

This book aims to present a collection of research papers which are related, in one way or another, to financial crises. The work contained herein ranges from topics such as the sources, origins and political and institutional dynamics of the global financial crisis we had during 2007/09 (GFC) to the liberalisation of economies, macroeconomic development, and the behaviour of interest and exchange rates during periods of political turmoil. Naturally, given its importance and far-reached economic, political and social effects across the globe, the majority of the chapters that will follow are related to the GFC. However, the timing of writing the introduction to this book is such that I strongly believe that the effects (and potential effects) on the financial system and banks of another crisis—a very different one—need to be addressed; I am referring of course to the ongoing economic crisis caused by the COVID-19 pandemic. As such, the prime aim of this chapter is to discuss the effects of this latter crisis on the global economy and the financial sector, in particular, and in doing so provide a 'bridge' between what is discussed in the chapters that follow and what is actually happening around us at this time.

The chapter unfolds as follows: Section 2 discusses the effect of the pandemic on the world economy and the financial system; Section 3 deals with the banking system; and Section 4 concludes.

2. The effect of COVID-19 on the world economy and the financial system

There is little doubt that the COVID-19 pandemic has caused an extraordinary human and health crisis. The measures taken by governments all over the world necessary to contain the virus have resulted in an economic downturn whose severity and length are still quite uncertain. Initially, the pandemic was seen as a China/Asian regional shock; however, very quickly, it became apparent that the virus was 'travelling' quickly and that the shock would indeed be a global one. It is now clear that the last time the world economy suffered such a shock was after the demise of Lehman Brothers in September 2008. Under this 'prism', Baldwin and Tomiura [1] point out that the GFC could provide a broad perspective on the range of likely outcomes this time around; more specifically, the authors refer to what came to be known as the 'great trade collapse', which was the steepest fall in world trade since the Great Depression (see **Figure 1**).

As far as global economic growth is concerned, recent IMF estimates [2] indicate a decline of 3% for 2020, which incidentally is worse than the one experienced during the GFC. At the same time, the timing and—importantly—the shape of a potential future recovery remain uncertain. Within this context, Mann [3] argues that this crisis will probably be a U-shaped one (rather than a V-shaped one), on the grounds of what happened as a result of other epidemics. Having said that, however, we need to stress out that, from an economic perspective (and not only), COVID-19 is different from other pandemics (Asian Flu, Hong-Kong Flu, Avian Flu, SARS, MERS, and Ebola Virus Disease), in the sense that they either 'hit' nations that were not so dominant economically or the number of registered cases was much smaller; we should not forget that the current pandemic has greatly affected the G7 plus China, among several other countries.

Given the above developments on world trade and economic growth, unavoidably the global financial system has also felt a dramatic impact with the asset prices falling sharply; actually, according to the IMF [2] (see **Figure 2**), several stock markets across the world experienced declines of 30% plus at the worst point of the sell-off (we should note that most of them have recovered since then). Moreover, worrying signs were also observed in important short-term funding markets, including that for US dollars, as well as other credit markets, with spreads rising substantially. The strain experienced by financial markets may also be seen through the volatility 'lenses', where spikes in volatility reached levels not seen since the GFC, reflecting the uncertainties caused by COVID-19 (see **Figure 3**).

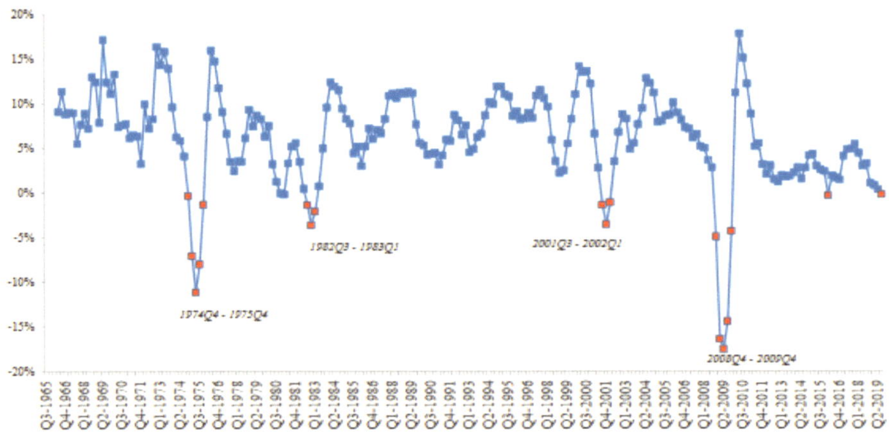

Figure 1.
Quarter-on-quarter growth, world imports volume, 1965–2019 Q3. Source: Baldwin and Tomiura, elaboration on WTO online data (www.WTO.org).

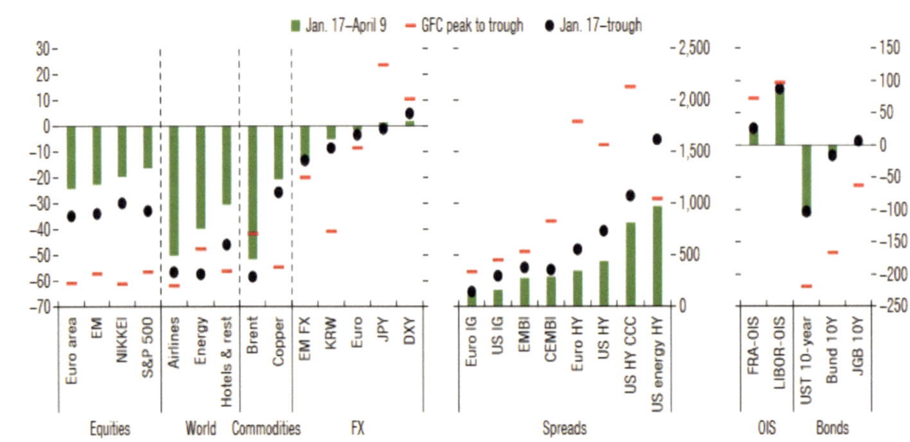

Figure 2.
Asset market performance as of April 9, 2020 (measured in percentage points and basis points). Source: IMF, global financial stability overview, April 2020.

Within the above framework, and given the need to stabilise the global financial system so as to support the real economy, as is often the case, central banks had to take bold action. To do this, they had to re-activate 'weapons' used during the course of the GFC in order to contain the upward pressures on the cost of credit and make sure that firms and households would have access to credit (at a reasonable price); effectively, central banks stepped in as 'buyers of the last resort' of risky assets, such as bonds issued by firms, including high-yield ones. Moreover, central banks in advanced economies cut interest rates to historically low levels (see **Figure 4**) while substantial interest rate cuts were also observed in emerging markets. Finally,

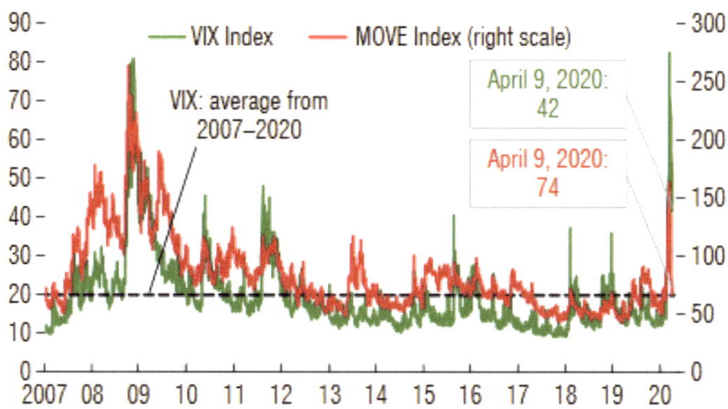

Figure 3.
Volatility indexes (measured in percentage points). Source: IMF, global financial stability overview, April 2020.

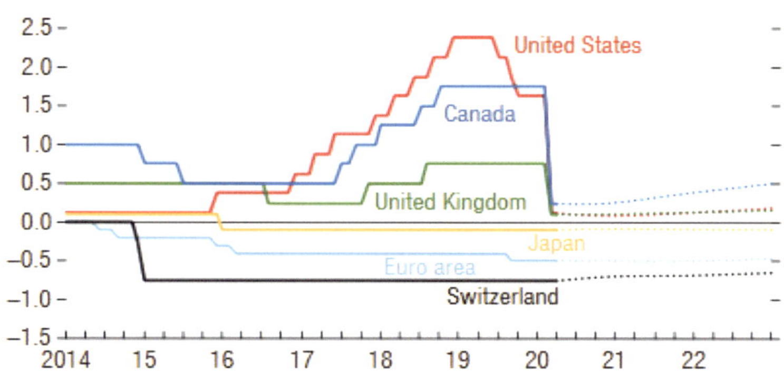

Figure 4.
Actual and expected policy rates. Source: IMF, global financial stability overview, April 2020.

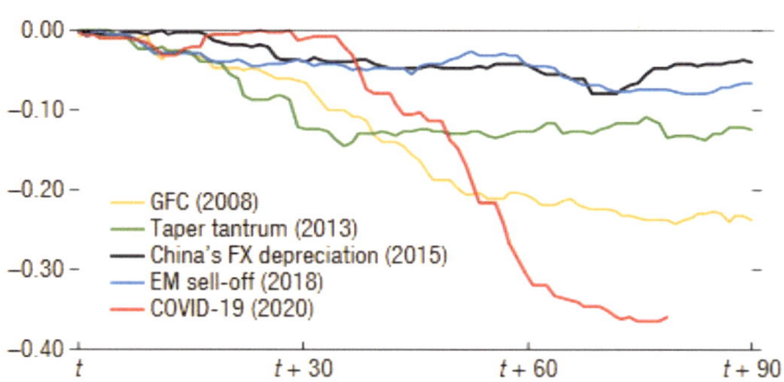

Figure 5.
Cumulative non-resident portfolio flows to emerging markets (% of GDP). Source: IMF, global financial stability overview, April 2020.

central banks have also provided liquidity to the financial system through Open Market Operations (OPM). These actions have certainly helped to 'calm' markets, some of which have substantially recovered lately; however, despite this, it should be noted that investor sentiment is still fragile.

Putting all the above together, the deterioration of the global economic outlook has dramatically changed the 1-year ahead projections of global economic growth; actually, according to the IMF [2], it has shifted it massively to the left (there is a 5% probability that it will fall below −7.4%; same as referring to an event that is expected to happen once every 20 years). It is quite possible that, as so often happens at times of financial crises, emerging markets are hit the hardest, since investors tend to withdraw their capital and look for so-called 'safe-haven' assets (**Figure 5** below 'speaks for itself').

3. What about banks?

From a historical point of view, some of the most striking examples of contagion in the financial sector have involved international banks; recall for example the GFC and the euro area crises, or the crisis in South East Asia in the late nineties, among many others[1]. According to Beck [5], this time banks are not likely to be a major 'channel' of transmission, due to the fact that adherence to stricter regulatory requirements in recent time has meant that their capital buffers are much stronger now, and the system—as a whole—is presumably safer. In particular, the author argues that in the case of European banks even under a scenario of an 8.3% decline in GDP over 3 years, banks would still be in good shape. Furthermore, the coordinated and substantial action by central banks in providing ample liquidity to banks in several countries has further 'insulated' the banking system, at least for now.

Nonetheless, others such as Cecchetti and Schoenholtz [6] appear to be more concerned in case there is a confidence crisis, which in turn might result in 'bank runs' that are, by definition, contagious; as the authors put it *The news about a run on a specific bank alerts everyone to the fact that there may be other 'lemons' among the universe of banks, turning a run into a panic.* As such, it is of paramount importance that people are well informed about the 'linkage' between the economic and the medical effects of the pandemic, so as not to over-react without reason; effectively, what we should be looking for are honest and transparent governments. Cochrane [7] 'paints' an even bleaker picture pointing out that 'shutting the economy down' could cause large financial problems related for example to companies that will have to continue paying their debts and bills and people that will have to pay rent or make mortgage payments; all this could lead to a wave of bankruptcies and insolvencies.

Eventually, how things will turn out for banks will depend, to a great extent, on how the situation evolves going forward; for example, if the global spread of COVID-19 requires imposing tougher containment measures, these are likely to lead to an even more severe economic downturn. Such a development would probably unveil crucial vulnerabilities of the financial system; for instance, investment managers are likely to face substantial capital outflows and thus will be forced to sell assets in falling markets thus accentuating the downward prices 'spiral'. At the same time, companies are more likely to face distress, with default rates rising; recall for instance what happened to Flybe, the UK airline, which struggled to meet

[1] A comprehensive discussion of international banking crises can be found in the work of Reinhart and Rogoff [4].

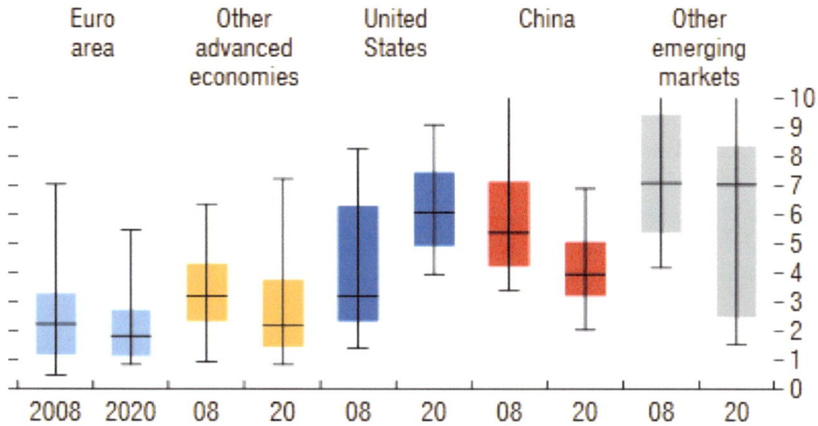

Figure 6.
Decline in bank market capitalisation. Source: IMF, global financial stability overview, April 2020.

its obligations and went into administration in early March, 2020. Events like this are likely to harm credit markets, especially their riskier parts (e.g. non-investment grade bonds).

If such a scenario was to unfold, despite the fact that banks have more capital and liquidity than in the past, it is plausible that their resilience might eventually be tested. Declines in asset prices are likely to result in losses in the investment portfolios of banks (especially with respect to risky assets), while rising bond yields for highly indebted governments might just remind us of the sovereign-financial sector nexus, which provided so much pain in the course of the euro area crisis. In addition, the longer the pause in economic activity, the more likely it is that the banking sector will register credit losses on their lending portfolios to companies and households, especially the more vulnerable ones (e.g. think of energy companies and falling oil prices or a shutdown factory that nonetheless still has to pay its workers and debt). Finally, lower bank profitability would imply—by default—that banks will have less income (and potentially reserves) against which to write-off losses resulting from the above.

Actually, looking at the market reaction of bank stock prices during the unfolding of the pandemic, we observe large declines, which indicate investor concern regarding the prospects of the sector. Interestingly, **Figure 6** seems to suggest that bank capitalisations fell more in 2020 than during the GFC in several parts of the world.

Given the above, financial regulators and supervisory authorities have taken some bold steps (in addition to those of central banks discussed in Section 2), which may be summarised as follows: (a) some countries have allowed banks to operate below their normal liquidity requirements and to utilise their capital conservation buffers[2]; (b) some countries have also adjusted (temporarily) their supervisory priorities and eased regulatory requirements (e.g. delay of stress-tests and flexibility in the treatment of non-performing loans); (c) restriction of bank dividend payouts. It is worth noting that similar measures have been taken to support other non-bank financial sector firms such as insurance companies and asset managers; for example, in the case of the latter, we have seen measures such as bans on short sales.

[2] According to the European Systemic Risk Board (ESRB), the capital conservation buffer is a capital buffer that equals 2.5% of a bank's total exposures that needs to be met with an additional amount of Common Equity Tier 1 capital. The buffer sits on top of the 4.5% minimum requirement for Common Equity Tier 1 capital.

4. Conclusion

Last time around, in the course of the GFC, world leaders moved together to provide a common, coordinated response to the crisis; it was probably not perfect, but eventually it worked. Today, global leaders are facing a similar, if not greater and more complex, challenge, and their 'measures' will be assessed by their ability to deal with this global threat. Obviously, priority should be given to the public health aspects of the virus and in containing as much as possible the pandemic.

Regarding the financial system, it is quite possible that COVID-19 could have important repercussions for banks and other financial institutions. On a positive note, these repercussions do not seem likely to be imminent, as banks are stronger this time around. This means that adequate preparation by the regulatory authorities is possible, without of course any room for complacency, as markets can react quickly, unpredictably and in a contagious manner. Within this context, according to Beck [5], regulatory authorities should focus on (and prepare for) the following: (1) possible operational disruptions in the financial system, (2) strengthening confidence in financial markets by clearly signalling that they stand ready to intervene (they have shown this intention to a great extent so far), and (3) preparing for possible interventions in and resolution of failing banks.

Beyond any doubt, the aforementioned and in particular the role of central banks will be very crucial to maintain stability in global financial markets and make sure that credit flows to the real economy. But we need to remember that this crisis is not only about liquidity, it is also about solvency; after all, large segments of the economies of many countries have come to a standstill. As such, fiscal policy also has a vital role to play, where along with monetary and other policies; they should provide a 'cushion' against the impact of the pandemic, paving the way for an economic recovery later on.

To conclude then, there are currently several questions of economic nature that are seeking answers, for example, how far will the economic damage go? How bad will things eventually get? What will be the extent of economic contagion? And, importantly, what can policy-makers do to alleviate it? And will it work? Unfortunately, we do not have answers to these questions, only time accompanied by good research will provide them. For sure, however, the crisis caused by COVID-19 will rightfully take its own place in the long list of economic and financial crisis, some of which are discussed in this book, and is likely to make interesting reading for future market analysts and policy-makers.

Author details

Stelios N. Markoulis
Cyprus International Institute of Management, University of Cyprus,
Open University of Cyprus, Cyprus

*Address all correspondence to: smarkoulis@cytanet.com.cy

References

[1] Baldwin R, Tomiura E. Thinking ahead about the trade impact of COVID-19, chapter 5. In: Baldwin R, Beatrice Weder di Mauro BW, editors. Economics in the Time of COVID-19. A VoxEU.org Book. CERP Press; 2020

[2] IMF. Global Financial Stability Overview. Washington DC; 2020

[3] Mann CL. Real and financial lenses to assess the economic consequences of COVID-19, chapter 5. In: Baldwin R, Beatrice Weder di Mauro BW, editors. Economics in the Time of COVID-19. A VoxEU.org Book; CERP Press; 2020

[4] Reinhart C, Rogoff K. This Time Is Different: Eight Centuries of Financial Folly. Princeton University Press; 2009

[5] Thorsten Beck T. Finance in the times of Corona virus, chapter 6. In: Baldwin R, Beatrice Weder di Mauro BW, editors. Economics in the Time of COVID-19. A VoxEU.org Book. CERP Press; 2020

[6] Cecchetti SG, Schoenholtz KL. Bank Runs and Panics: A Primer. Available from: www.moneyandbanking.com. 2020

[7] Cochrane. Corona virus monetary policy, chapter 12. In: Baldwin R, Beatrice Weder di Mauro BW, editors. Economics in the Time of COVID-19. A VoxEU.org Book. CERP Press; 2020

Section 2

Origin of the Financial Crisis

Chapter 2

The Primary Origin of the Financial Crisis

Aloui Mouna and Jarboui Anis

Abstract

This paper examines the relationship between the stock return volatility, outside directors, independent directors, and variable control using simultaneous-equation panel data models for a panel of 89 France-listed companies on the SBF 120 over the period of 2006–2012. Our results showed that the outside directors (FD) and audit size increase the stock return volatility. Furthermore, the results indicate that the independent directors and ROA have a negative effect on the stock return volatility; this result indicates that these variables contribute to decrease and stabilize the stock return volatility. This study employs a variety of econometric models, including feedback, to test the robustness of our empirical results. Also, we examine the relationship between the corporate governance and the stock returns volatility, exchange rate, and treasury bill using GARCH-BEKK model for a panel of 99 French firms over the period of 2006–2013.

Keywords: stock return volatility, corporate governance, risk management, simultaneous-equation models, GARCH

1. Introduction

During the peak of the global financial crisis of 2008, the major failures that have been involved in the banking crisis were particularly remuneration, as executive incentives, risk management, shareholder activism, and the problems of qualification of the board. Indeed, an excess of credit combined with poor governance in the banking industry can generate carrier failures of a systematic risk. At this point, the term governance has drawn the attention of lawyers and economics experts, political scientists, sociologists, and management scientists [1]. Also, poor banking governance was a major cause of global crisis [2].

Bernanke [3] showed that the financial crisis of 2007/2008 has been started for many reasons (insufficient information, fraud, and incompetence).

Kirkpatrick [4] suggests that the systematic crisis, due to the failure of the international financial market, was also a crisis of corporate governance and regulations. Before and during the financial crisis, corporate governance issues have been attracted attention, since it led to the collapse of many financial institutions in the OECD report. Kirkpatrick [4] showed that the "financial crisis can be to an important extent attributed to failures and weakness of corporate governance arrangements. When they were put to the test, corporate governance routines did not serve the purpose to safeguard against excessive risk-taking in some financial service companies."

IntechOpen

Furthermore, the subprime crisis started in the second half of 2006 with the crash of mortgage loans (mortgages) at risk in the United States (the subprime), which borrowers, often of a modest condition, were no longer able to repay. Revealed in February 2007 by the announcement of significant provisions passed by the HSBC bank, it turned into an open crisis when the periodic auctions did not find buyers in July 2007. Given the current accounting rules, it is impossible to give a value to these securities, which had to be provisioned at a value close to zero.

Besides, policy makers have realized the extent and nature of this crisis belatedly, during the collapse of the prices of the various assets. The recent "subprime" crisis revealed some shortcomings in corporate governance and risk management. It also revealed failures of risk management throughout the business world. Since corporate governance is designed to reduce the information asymmetry and control of opportunism management, which is considered as a factor, this contributed to the recent crisis [5, 6]. The latter is crucial for both the developed and developing countries. The organization of power in the company is considered an important factor in the stability of capital markets and investment dynamics.

In fact, risk management is widespread as a mode of governance and management control, although financial crisis has clearly shown its shortcomings. Based on the existing literature on risk management, we will argue that the global financial crisis provides ample opportunity to understand the rhetorical tactics informing about the discourse of risk management. Our research is based on a scientific debate about the relationship between risk management and corporate governance. Several studies showed that corporate governance failure and risk management are the primary causes of the 2008–2009 crisis. Inadequate risk management and inappropriate remuneration practices in the financial sector are placed squarely in the center of the financial crisis. Risk management presents the most important factor in the context of a set of practices and corporate governance structures. While most studies indicate that the weakness o corporate governance and inadequate risk management leads to the financial crisis, in particular, where there is insufficient risk oversight by the board of directors. For example, Working Group on Financial Regulation (2008)[1] mention in March just before the Bear Stearns collapse, "risk management feebleness at some large US and European financial institutions" as one of "the primary underlying causes of the turmoil in the financial markets." That report complains about "regulatory policies, including capital and disclosure requirements that failed to mitigate risk management weaknesses." They showed that the weak risk management in some major US and European financial institutions was the main causes of the global financial crisis. Other investigations indicate that the defeat in corporate governance is a major factor in the financial crisis.

In this chapter, we focus on the French market and bring new light in various regards.

First, France is based on concentration ownership, marked by family stockholders, even big, public companies [7]. In this area, Faccio and Lang [8] indicate that less than 14% of French companies are multi-participation, against to 37% in Europe in general; furthermore, 64.82% of French companies are controlled by a single family, compared to 44.29% in Europe. Also, Johnson et al. [9], France is different to other European countries, in the financial systems, since it comprises two systems, which are the following ones: "the central family" and the "based on the bank," although the first prevails.

---

[1] See The President's Working Group on Financial Markets, "Policy Statement on Financial Markets," March 2008, https://ecgi.global/sites/default/files/working_papers/documents/SSRN-id1448118.pdf

Second, the legal context is also unique: France is based on civil law, with little protection for minority shareholders, a weak market for corporate control and very few hostile takeovers [10].

2. Literature review

2.1 Does corporate governance "cause" the financial crisis

Walker's review [11] showed that the moral failure and inadequacy of corporate governance mechanisms in the global financial system contribute to the financial crises.

In this vein, Minton [12], Lemmon and Lins [13], and Baek et al. [14] found that a certain degree of corporate governance is effective regarding the stock price reduction in the event of a financial crisis. However, risk is another important factor on which investors base their investment. Therefore, Huson et al. and Choi et al. [15, 16] stated that higher ratio of independent directors is expected to have a positive effect on corporate performance. Huang et al. [17] believe that the independent board can help reduce the stock market volatility. They divide the sample into two groups regarding whether the firm appoints independent directors and investigate the effect of independent directors on stock price volatility.

Burcu et al. [18] showed that the interaction of ownership structures and stock prices differ from period to period. They indicated the positive relation between inside ownership structure and stock price in the periods January 2008 and March 2009; a negative relationship is observed during the periods between October 2008 and January 2009. The strong negative relation is monitored between largest ownership, concentrated ownership, and stock prices.

Steven [19] uses a variety of econometric models, including feedback, to test the robustness of (dynamic panel estimations) and to examine the relationship between the board's characteristics and foreign ownership. They showed that the outside directors have important role in the stabilized stock price volatility.

2.2 Risk management and the financial crisis

Karolyi et al. [20] indicated that the yen/dollar foreign exchange rates, the treasury bill returns, and the industry impacts have no measurable effect on the US and Japanese return correlations. Moreover, Antoniou et al. [21, 22] found that futures' trading has a significant impact on co-movements across the markets. Borokhovich et al. [23] found that there is a positive nexus between the monitoring of outside directors and the firm's use of the interest rate derivatives.

2.3 Risk management, corporate governance

Board sizes are responsible for the identification, assessment, and management of all types of risk, including operational risk, market risk, and liquidity risk (FRC2010b). The debate regarding this relationship, which has long been ignored as an important element in the process of development of the stock markets, minimizes the risk of investor. In this context, Minton et al. [12] found that the board size negatively affects the market risk. Similarly, in a recent study, Kryvko et al. [24] have examined the European banks and also found a negative relationship between the board size and the risk of the company.

Regarding the relationship between the independence of the board and the risk of liquidity, the first who examined the debate were Anderson et al. [25], who used the cost of the debt of the company as a proxy. They found that the more independent board is, the more the debt cost decreases. Pathan [26] found that the independent board is negatively associated with the market risk.

3. Results

3.1 Corporate governance stock returns volatility

3.1.1 Methodology and data

In this paper, we examine the three-way linkages between corporate governance and stock return volatility. Our study focuses on French companies composing the SBF 120 index for the data collection; we were required to use a data source, i.e., the database "http://investir.lesechos.fr." The sample period runs from 2006 to 2012.

The following regression equation is formulated to test empirically the

$$\begin{aligned} VOL_i &= \alpha + \beta_1 CEO_i + \beta_2\, FD_i + \beta_3\, INDD_i + \beta_4\, CPA_i \\ &\quad + \beta_5\ LEV_i + \beta_6\, SIZE_i + \beta_7 PER_i + \beta_8 TURN_i + \varepsilon_i \end{aligned} \tag{1}$$

The *Vol*, as the dependent variable in the model, is measured by the standard deviation of annual stock returns. Concerning the independent variable is as follows:

The *CEO* is the chairman also serving as CEO. The *INDD* is independent directors and measured by the ratio of independent directors. The *FD* is outside directors. The *CPA* is audit size.

In addition, the variable of corporate governance is as follows: *PER* is ROA. The *TURN* is firm size (total liabilities). The *SIZE* is firm size, and the *LEV* is firm's debt ratio. Our work is a panel data study, Eq. (1) can be written in the form of panel data as follows:

$$VOL_{it} = \alpha + \alpha_i + \sum_j \beta_j E_{jit} + \sum_n \delta_n Y_n + \varepsilon_{it} \tag{2}$$

Since our study is a panel data study, Eq. (3) can be written in a panel data form as follows:

$$VOL_{it} = \alpha + \alpha_i + \sum_{j-1} \beta_j E_{jit} + \sum_n \delta_n Y_n + \varepsilon_{it} \tag{3}$$

$$VOL_{it} = \alpha + VOL_{it} + \beta_{vd} INDD_{it} + \beta_{vf} FD + \beta_{vv} V_{i,t-1} + \sum_n \delta_n Y_n + \varepsilon_{it} \tag{4}$$

$$INDD_{it} = \alpha + \alpha_i INT_{it} + \beta_{vd} VOL_{it} + \beta_{vf} FD + \beta_{vv} INDD_{i,t-1} + \sum_n \delta_n Y_n + \varepsilon_{it} \tag{5}$$

$$FD_{it} = \alpha + \alpha_i FD_{it} + \beta_{vd} VOL_{it} + \beta_{vf} INDD + \beta_{vv} FD_{i,t-1} + \sum_n \delta_n Y_n + \varepsilon_{it} \tag{6}$$

We then use the production function in Eq. (4) to derive the empirical models to simultaneously examine the interactions between stock return volatility; INDD is independent directors, and FD is outside directors. These simultaneous-equation models are also constructed on the basis of the theoretical and empirical insights from the existing literature. While estimating the causal links between CEO is chairman also serving as CEO, CPA is audit size, PER is ROA, LEV is debt ratio, and SIZE is firm size are included as instrumental variables (e.g., [17, 27]).

In Eq. (5), INDD: present the independent directors CEO is chairman also serving as CEO, FD is outside.

Directors, and VOL is stock return volatility, are the main factors of resistance of the company during the variations of the stock markets.

In this research, we use a dynamic panel data model of lagged levels of the dependent variables and for this reason; we utilize the Blundell and Bond [28] two-step system GMM methodology. This methodology is explained on the basis that traditional OLS estimator is biased in the presence of the lagged-dependent variable as regressor, and it also reports for the prospective endogeneity of certain dependent variables.

3.1.2 Empirical result and discussion

Table 1 presents the descriptive statistics for the regression variables. In this table, we can see "Mean", "standard deviation", "Min", and "Max". The stock return volatility showed the maximum standard deviation 1.67%, and there is also a much smaller standard deviation of 0.003%, with a mean of 39.86% and a maximum of 1.16%. For an independent variable, the chairman also serving as CEO showed the maximum standard deviation of 48.16%, and there is also a much smaller standard deviation of 0%, with a mean of 63.56% and a maximum of 1%.

The independent directors showed the maximum standard deviation of 13.32%, and there is also a much smaller standard deviation of 0%, with a mean of 1.04% and a maximum of 33.3%. The outside directors illustrate the standard deviation of 18.58%, and there is also a much smaller standard deviation of 5.55%, with a mean of 29.16% and a maximum of 1.60%.

Concerning the control variable, the audit size showed the maximum standard deviation of 13.52%, with a mean of 32.96% and a maximum of 1.2%. The debt ratio presents the maximum standard deviation of 81.03%, with a mean of 53.09% and a maximum of 65.553%. For the firm's size showed a standard deviation of 79.27%, with a mean of 6.48% and a maximum of 8.90%. We can see "Mean", "standard deviation", "Min", and "Max". Finally, the ROA presents the maximum standard deviation of 57.01%, and there is also a much smaller standard deviation of −6.95%, with a mean of 7.27% and a maximum of 9.28%.

Next, **Table 2** provides the correlation matrix for the dependent variable, stock return volatility, and all the independent variables. It also presents the correlation coefficients among the variables in our analysis. At first glance, it can be seen that

Variables	Obs	Mean	Std. dev.	Min	Max
Stock return volatility	623	0.3986773	0.1878925	0.0037603	1.167427
Chairman also serving as CEO	623	0.635634	0.4816386	0	1
Outsider directors (FD)	367	0.291568	0.1858492	0.055555	1.609438
Independent directors	623	1.04751	13.32312	0	0.333
Audit size	623	0.3296789	0.1352636	0	1.2
Relative ROA	623	0.072706	0.5701465	−6.95	9.285
Debit ratio	623	53.09744	81.03811	−110.45	65.553
Firm size	623	6.483938	0.7927428	0	8.904955

Table 1.
Summary statistics of corporate governance.

Variables	Volatility	CEO	FD	IND	Audit size	ROA	Debt ratio	Firm size
Stock return volatility	1.000							
Chairman also serving as CEO	0.1286* 0.0013	1.000						
Outside directors (FD)	0.0445 0.3950	0.0846 0.1055	1.000					
Independent directors	−0.0132 0.7419	0.0287 0.4753	0.1974* 0.0001	1.000				
Audit size	0.0953* 0.0174	0.0207 0.6057	0.3308* 0.0000	−0.0456 0.2560	1.000			
Relative ROA	−0.0119 0.7674	0.0119 0.7676	0.0912 0.0811	−0.0034 0.9323	0.0073 0.8549	1.000		
Debt ratio	0.1199* 0.0027	0.0866* 0.0307	−0.0846 0.1055	−0.0341 0.3949	−0.0051 0.8999	0.0012 0.9760	1.000	
Firm size	−0.0019 0.9632	−0.0584 0.1452	−0.0451 0.3893	−0.0084 0.8341	−0.3175* 0.0000	0.0201 0.6174	0.0534 0.1827	1.000

The * indicate significance at the percent levels.

Table 2.
The correlation matrix of corporate governance.

Volatility stock return				
Variables	**Ols-Fe**	**Ols-Ar**	**Ab**	**Abbb**
Volatility stock return	0.0213691	0.0261624	−0.000477	−0.012617
Chairman also serving as CEO	0.0164611	0.1483642	0.2842368**	0.16203
Outside directors (FD)	0.1834594*	0.1840265**	0.2219233**	0.2840837**
Independent directors	0.0446437	0.0539175	−0.080685	0.1292659
Audit size	−0.042662	−0.075450	0.0526602	−0.209908***
Relative ROA	0.0002644*	0.0002502**	0.0001734	0.0003577**
Debt ratio	0.0043407	0.0064761	−0.008987	0.0338603
Firm size	0.0046849	0.018764	0.0280472	0.0128239
Constant	0.1674346	0.013684	−0.351875***	−0.1473147
Volatility		0.4377655*	0.2849317*	

The *, **, and *** significant at 1, 5, 10, percent levels, respectively.

Table 3.
Robustness tests—no feedback and governance variables not endogenous.

the stock price fluctuation is negatively correlated with the independent directors, relative ROA, and firm size which suggests that these variables help stabilize the stock return volatility. The stock price volatility is a positive correlation between the debt ratio, CEO, outside director, and audit size. In fact, all these have contributed to the increase of the stock price volatility.

In **Table 3**, we based on four methods (Ols-Fe, Ols-Ar, Ab, Abbb). Concerning the first method (OLS-fe), we can see only that the chairman also serving as CEO and relative ROA have a positive and significant (at 1%) impact on the stock market volatility, while the second method (OLS-ar), this result indicates that the CEO and ROA have a positive and significant (at 5%) impact on the stock market volatility. Concerning the Arellano-Bond regression (AB) method, we note that the CEO and outside directors have a positive and significant (at 1%) impact on the stock market volatility. This result suggests that these variables contribute to the increase in the stock return volatility.

The empirical results about Arellano-Bover/Blundell-Bond (ABBB) method showed that the outside directors and ROA have a positive and significant impact on the stock return volatility. Also, in this method we can see that the audit size have a negative and significant impact on the stock return volatility. This result suggests that the audit size contribute to decrease and reduce stock return volatility. Moreover, the different reports about robust regressions (OLS-fe, OLS-ar, ABBB, and AB) pointed out that the debt ratio (LEV) has a positive and significant impact on the stock market volatility. This suggests that the stock return volatility is elastic on the leverage ratio, and a 10% increase in the leverage ratio increases the stock return volatility within a range of 0.026%. This result indicates that the debt ratio increases the stock return volatility.

Table 4 presents the random effect regression effects. The first model (1) included only the control variable; the result indicates that the ROA has a positive and significant impact on the stock return volatility, while the firm size has a negative and significant impact on the stock return volatility. For model (2) that contains the dependent variable, we can see that the outside directors have a negative and significant impact on the stock return volatility; the outside directors can help to reduce the stock return volatility. According to Vo [29], the foreign director can stabilize the stock return volatility.

In model (3), when combining control variable with outside directors and independent directors, we found that the ROA has a positive and significant impact on the stock return volatility, while the firm size has a negative and significant impact on the stock return volatility. Finally, model (4) included all variables; the result indicates that the outside directors and ROA have a positive and significant impact on the stock return volatility.

In **Table 5**, we can see that the CEO, audit size, debt ratio, and total liabilities have statically significant and positive impacts on the stock return volatility; this result indicates that these variables contribute to increase the stock return volatility. Moreover, the fact that foreign ownership, firm's size, and ROA have a negative

Variables	Stock return volatility			
	Model 1	Model 2	Model 3	Model 4
Stock return volatility		0.0152933		0.0213691
Chairman also serving as CEO		0.0171294		0.0164611
Outside directors (FD)		0.1786031*	−0.0000928	0.1834594*
Independent directors		−0.0340352	−0.0337171	0−4.42e-10
Audit size	−0.0063078		−0.0063206	−0.0426624
Relative ROA	0.0002156***		0002145***	0.0002644***
Debt ratio	−0.0012812		−0.0012117	0.0043407
Firm size	−0.052031**		−0.051979**	0.0046849
Constant	0.7526633*		0.7519738*	0.1674346
Fixed/random effect	4.80	1.88	4.75	42.55*
Breusch-Pagan LM test (p-value)	789.20*	793.62*	789.37*	

*The *, **, and *** significant at 1, 5, 10, percent levels, respectively.*

Table 4.
Random effect regressions (the impact of corporate governance on the stock returns volatility).

Variables				
Volatility stock return	**Coef.**	**Std. Err.**	**t**	**P > |t|**
Chairman also serving as CEO	0.0314574***	0.0169676	1.85	0.065
Outsider directors (FD)	−0.0590011**	0.0526383	−1.12	0.026
Independent directors	0.0666269	0.0410113	1.62	0.105
Audit size	0.164201**	0.082536	1.99	0.047
Relative ROA	−0.352634*	0.1010953	−3.49	0.001
Debt Ratio	0.0004149*	0.0000889	4.67	0.000
Firm size	−0.0386955**	0.0123863	−3.12	0.002
Constant	0.0506746**	0.0179811	2.82	0.005

*The *, **, and *** significant at 1, 5, 10, percent levels, respectively.*

Table 5.
Linear regression.

Variables	(1)	(2)	(3)
	Volatility stock return	**FDi (outside directors)**	**IND (independent directors)**
Stock return volatility		0.997335	−0.088921*
Chairman also serving as CEO	−0.0024182	0.0150367	−0.0204414
Outsider directors (FD)	0.2347926**		0.3823154*
Independent directors	−0.9719472*	0.2.198526*	
Audit size	0.3733843**		
Relative ROA	−0.4283953**		
Debt ratio	0.0002094	−0.0002125	−0.0001434
Firm size		−0.0631012	0.0670512*
AR (1)	−3.28*	−2.34**	−3.04**
Test de Hansen	32.88**	10.28	13.09
Wu-Hausman F test	12.17108 F (1365)		
0.00054	22.59621 F (1365)		
0.00000	12.85766 F (1365)		
0.00038			
Durbin-Wu-Hausman	11.87514*	21.45378*	12.52223*

*The *, **, and *** significant at 1, 5, 10, percent levels, respectively.*

Table 6.
Three-stage least squares for simultaneous equations.

effect on the stock return volatility; these results indicate that these variables contribute to decrease and stabilize the stock return volatility.

Table 6 contains three-stage least squares for simultaneous equations. In this table, the result suggests that the outside directors (FD) and audit size have a positive and significant impact on the stock return volatility; this result indicates that these variables contribute to increase and stabilize the stock return volatility. In this area, this result compared to the study of Steven et al. [19], they indicate that the outside directors contribute to stabilize the stock return volatility. Also, we found the independent directors and ROA have a negative effect on the stock return volatility; this result indicates that these variables contribute to decrease and stabilize the stock return volatility.

Moreover, the results indicate that the stock return volatility has a negative and significant (1%) impact on the independent directors. This stipulates that the independent directors contributed to the minimization of the volatility of the stock returns, that is to say, they are considered a real factor of corporate governance. In this context, the independent directors are considered a sign of good governance. This result is consistent with the findings of Huang et al. [17].

Table 6 reports the results of Arellano and Bover [30] and Blundell and Bond [28] "system GMM" estimation of [Eq. (2)], using different measures of the firm. In the GMM system, first-differenced variables are used as instruments for the equations in levels, and the estimates are robust to unobserved heterogeneity, simultaneity, and dynamic endogeneity (if any). The diagnostic tests in **Table 5** show that the model [Eq. (2)] presenting the effect of the stock return fluctuation on the independent director is well-fitted with statistically insignificant test statistics of the first-order autocorrelation in first differences (AR1) and Hansen J-statistics of overidentifying restrictions. Accordingly, in **Table 5**, we could see statistically insignificant AR (1) for all the firm's measures. Likewise, the Hansen's J-statistics of overidentifying restriction test, the null instrument validity, and the statistically insignificant Hansen J-statistics for all the firm's measures indicate that the instruments are valid in the respective estimation. Finally, the number of instruments (i.e., 24) used in the model is less than the panel (i.e., 212) which makes the Hansen J-statistics more reliable. By contrast, Eq. (1) presents the impact of the independent directors on the stock price fluctuation and shows that it is well fitted with the statistically significant test statistics of the first-order autocorrelation in the first differences of AR (1) and with the Hansen J-statistics of overidentifying restrictions.

3.2 Risk management and the financial crisis

3.2.1 Data description and variable

In this paper, we examine the linkages between stock returns and risk management. Our study focuses on French companies composing the SBF 120 index for the data collection; we were required to use a data source, i.e., the database "http://investir.lesechos.fr." The sample period runs from 2006 to 2013.

3.2.1.1 Stock returns volatility

Annual returns are computed as geometric and arithmetic growth rates, respectively. In particular, we used the formula $\frac{P_t - P_{t-1}}{P_{t-1}}$ for the annual data.

3.2.1.2 Exchange rate

The study is an extension of the approach suggested by Karolyi et al. [20], Longin and Solnik [31] to examine the future contracts (such as foreign exchange rates, treasury bond, and index of stock prices).

3.2.1.3 Treasury bills

This measure has been used in the previous studies, including those of Koulakiotis et al. [32]. We want to help enrich the earlier work by studying French companies.

3.2.1.4 Market index

This variable was also considered by Zhian et al. [33] and Koulakiotis et al. [32].

3.2.2 Model

$$FD_{it} = \alpha + \alpha_i FD_{it} + \beta_{vd} VOL_{it} + \beta_{vf} INDD + \beta_{vv} FD_{i,t-1} + \sum_n \delta_n Y_n + \varepsilon_{it} \quad (7)$$

In **Table 7,** we can see all that the maximum standard deviation of the stock returns in the financial crisis in our sample is 73%, and there is also a much smaller standard deviation of 37%. These results show that the great impact of the financial crisis on all firm's stock price volatility.

Table 8 shows the correlations of all the variables. In this table, it can be seen that the stock return volatility is negatively correlated with the exchange rates, which suggests that the exchange rate variables help stabilize the stock return volatility. The stock return volatility is also positively correlated with the treasury bills.

In **Table 9,** the results confirm that an exchange rate is negatively and significantly correlated with the stock return volatility. Moreover, the treasury bills

Variable	Obs	Mean	Std. Dev.	Min	Max
Stock returns volatility	986	0.6748399	0.8306421	0	7.307498
Exchange rates	986	2.006649	0.0063299	1.997008	2.019531
Treasury bills	986	2.734162	0.5490697	2.09	3.72

Table 7.
Summary statistics of management risk.

Variables	Stock returns volatility	Exchange rates	treasury Bills
Stock returns volatility	1.0000		
Exchange rates	−0.0613	1.0000	
Treasury bills	0.0032	0.6833	1.0000

Table 8.
The correlation matrix of management risk.

Stock returns volatility	Coef.	Std. Err.	P > |t|
Exchange rates	−15.62909	5.710487	0.006
Treasury bills	0.1279229	0.0658331	0.052
Cons	31.68719	11.33675	0.005

Table 9.
Summary statistics of risk management and the financial crisis.

have a positive effect on the stock return volatility, which is clearly evidenced in all the regressions.

3.3 Risk management and corporate governance

3.3.1 Data description and variable

3.3.1.1 Dependent variables

In this paper, we examine the three-way linkages between stock returns, corporate governance, and risk management. Our study focuses on French companies composing the SBF 120 Index For the data collection; we were required to use a data source, i.e., the database "http://investir.lesechos.fr." The sample period runs from 2006 to 2013. Annual returns are computed as geometric and arithmetic growth rates, respectively. In particular, we used the formula $\frac{P_t - P_{t-1}}{P_{t-1}}$ for the annual data.

3.3.1.2 Independent variables

- Board of directors

The board of directors is an important internal mechanism in business that contributes to the control of management. In this sense, several authors consider that a large board strengthens its ability to control and improve its information sources. In this context, several studies found that companies with a large board of directors are realizing better performance (Daily and Dalton) [34]. Hence, we set the following assumption:

H1: The impact of the board is positive on the stock market volatility

- Institutional investors

Institutional investors have an active role in corporate governance. In this sense, Pound [35] pointed out that institutional shareholders are better equipped regarding knowledge and monitoring of professional skills than individual shareholder. In this way, the agency problems can be reduced. Current research also supports the monitoring mechanism on the part of institutional investors [36, 37]. Moreover, institutional control also plays an important role in the company's performance. Cornett et al. [38] reported that institutional investors have a positive influence on the performance of a company. Sias and Starks [39] found that higher institutional shareholdings would have a positive impact on stock prices. On the other hand, Dennis et al. [40] showed that abnormal stock returns during periods of high market volatility linked to the percentage of institutional ownership could be used to predict abnormal stock returns during the liquidity crisis. Beber et al. [41] found that institutional ownership affects liquidity. To do this, we put forward the following hypothesis:

H2: The impact of institutional investors is negative on the stock market volatility

- Exchange rate

The study is an extension of the approach suggested by Karolyi [20], Longin, and Solnik [31] to examine the future contracts (such as foreign exchange rates, treasury bond, and index of stock prices). To this end, we propose the following hypothesis:

H3: The exchange rate impact is positive on the stock market volatility

- Market index:

A hint of what is designed to measure price changes of a set of markets, such as the stock market or the bond market. This variable was also considered by Zhian et al. [32] and Koulakiotis et al. [33].

H4: The impact of the market index on the stock market volatility is positive

3.3.2 Model

3.3.2.1 GARCH model

Eqs. (8) and (9) show the return and volatility equations, respectively, which have been used in the investigation of the impact of corporate governance variables on the volatility persistence and error terms. Accordingly, the corporate governance variables are embedded in the model below to detect the effect on volatility and error:

$$\begin{aligned} r_t &= \beta_0 + \beta_1 s_1 + \beta_2 s_2 + \varepsilon_t \\ \varepsilon_t/\pi_{t-1} &\sim T(0, h_t) \end{aligned} \tag{8}$$

s_1 denotes the variable of corporate governance of the average board size. The second corporate governance variable s_2 controls the share of employee representatives. The sample period is from 2006 to 2013. A symmetric response to shocks is made from Bollerslev's univariate GARCH model:

$$h_t = \alpha_0 + \alpha_1 h_1 + \alpha_2 \varepsilon_{t-1}^2 \tag{9}$$

3.3.3 Empirical results and discussions

Table 10 reports the summary statistics and the diagnostic tests of AR (1) residuals. We can observe that the results uncover non-normality since the Jarque-Bera test rejects the null hypothesis of Gaussianity at 1% level. The series also displays a negative skewness and leptokurtic behavior, symptomatic of a heavier tailed distribution than the standard.

The descriptive statistics of the different variables for the panel are given in **Table 1**.

From **Table 1**, we find that the coefficients of skewness are positive in some cases and negative in others; it is to that the distribution of the variables is shifted left asymmetric for some variables (board of administration) and right for other

	Mean	Variance	Skewness	Kurtosis	Jarque-Bera
SBF120	0.169785	0.851913	6.300151	61.426594	56358.580960
Institutional investors	0.377604	0.085123	0.484719	−0.907466	25.274010
Exchange rate	2.007108	0.000049	0.454862	−0.623050	17.426292
Board size	1.090817	0.020644	−0.772521	1.339174	59.921052

Table 10.
Summary statistics of corporate governance and risk management.

variables. It may be noted that the lowest coefficients of negative skewness are recorded for boards of directors, while the highest skewness is recorded in the case of returns SBF120.

The coefficients of kurtosis variables are significantly more than three (SBF 120). This shows that for these series, which have a flatter distribution than the normal distribution, all other distributions are leptokurtic. According to the test Jarque-Bera (JB), the null hypothesis (H_0) of normality is not rejected, and the different variables studied are not normally distributed.

Table 11 shows the correlations of all the variables. We observe any high correlations among the independent variables that might affect our regression results. This table shows the correlations between all the variables. We observe high correlations among the independent variables that might affect our regression results.

Table 12 shows the results of the panel unit root tests for the levels of the variables. It can be seen from **Table 12** that all the variables in first difference are statistically significant under the LLC and HLM tests, indicating that all variables are integrated of order one, I(1). Furthermore, the results shown in the table indicate that all the series that display values LLC and HLM are below the critical values. Therefore, we accept hypothesis H1. The variables of this study are stationary and integrated of order zero because there is no differentiation for the first stationary.

In **Table 13**, we can observe that the results uncover non-normality since both the Ljung-Box (Q(10)) and the Breusch-Godfrey LM statistics point to the absence of autocorrelation in the residual series, which reveals that the chosen AR (1) specification seems sufficient to eliminate any serial correlation present in the data. Our results showed the stationarity constraint of the model is verified ($\alpha + \beta < 1$) for all the equations, which supports a weak presence of effect ARCH and GARCH

Variables	SBF 120	Exchange rate	Board size	INST INV
SBF120	1.000000	−0.0392 0.4686	−0.0569 0.2930	0.0809 0.1345
Exchange rate		1.000000	−0.0569 0.2930	0.0108 0.8420
Board size			1.000000	0.0539 0.3188
Institutional investors				1.00000

Table 11.
The correlation matrix of corporate governance and risk management.

Variables	First level	
	LLC	HLM
SBF120	−9.8018 (0.0000)	1.3191 0.0936
Exchange rate	−17.4655 (0.0000)	6.0866 (0.0000)
Institutional investors	−25.5105 (0.0000)	2.9574 (0.0016)
Board size	−1.1e + 02 (0.0000)	7.0130 (0.0000)

Table 12.
Unit root test based on levels of variables for all four panels.

Variables	c	AR_1	α_0	α_1	β_1	AIC(6)	BIC(6)	Ljung-Box	Pop
SBF120	0.1156 0.0970	0.7141 0.000	473.83 0.003	0.1208 0.000	0.7621 0.000	3836.10	3859.13	304	0
Exchange rate	0.5464 0.0000	−0.9764 0.00000	0.2086 0.0000	−0.4196 0.000	0.8922 0.000	1250.59	1273.61	5.69	0
Board size	0.02216 0.000	0.80378 0.0000	0.0586 0.0000	56.68195 0.0000	0.75636 0.0000	3003.86	3026.89	7089	0
Institutional investors	0.08737 0.76299	0.79627 0.000	6052.5 0.1325	0.32979 0.07420	0.56896 0.04523	4288.42	4311.44	156,124	0

Table 13.
Univariate GARCH effects with and without the impact of corporate governance variables.

in all the cases (exchange rate and institutional investor), except for (board size, SBF120), i.e., ($\alpha + \beta$) ≥ 1 has a high persistence of volatility shocks. So, in this we can see that the institutional investors reduce their stock price volatility.

4. Conclusion

This study investigated the relationship between the internal mechanisms of corporate governance and the stock return volatility on panel data models of 89 firms over the period of 2006–2012.

Concerning the relation between the internal mechanisms of corporate governance and stock return volatility, our results based on the three-stage least squares for simultaneous equations, in this area we can see that the outside directors (FD) and audit size have a positive and significant impact on the stock return volatility, and our results showed that the outside directors (FD) and audit size increase the stock return volatility. Also, we found that the independent directors and ROA have a negative effect on the stock return volatility; this result indicates that these variables contribute to decrease and stabilize the stock return volatility.

For the linkages between stock returns volatility and risk management (exchange rate, treasury bills), our study focuses on French companies composing the SBF 120 during 2006–2013. Our results confirm that an exchange rate is negatively and significantly correlated with the stock return volatility. This result indicates that these variables contribute to decrease and stabilize the stock return volatility. Moreover, the treasury bills have a positive effect on the stock return volatility.

Our results showed that the stationarity constraint of the model is verified ($\alpha + \beta < 1$) for all the equations, which supports a weak presence of effect ARCH and GARCH in all the cases except for stock index, board of directors, and inv. inst., i.e., ($\alpha + \beta$) ≥ 1 has a high persistence of volatility shocks.

The principal connotation, which occurs from our study, can be posted as follows. The results of this paper are particularly important for research on institutional investor in the French markets and the firm's stock price fluctuation. This paper provides evidence that confirms the benefits of institutional investors in the French markets. Moreover, the finding in this paper suggests that intuitional investors in France are beneficial for the economy not only because for their contribution to the invested firms but also due to the stabilizing effect benefits in macroeconomic perspectives. This paper also has clear policy implications for the government. Firstly, it provides an empirical investigation to clarify the role of the institutional investor's participation. It clearly suggests that the existence of more institutional investors in firms reduce their stock price volatility, and hence, they become less stock market's volatility. Secondly, a clear understanding of the stock market volatility and effects of institutional investors is important for policy makers in making relevant policies on foreign capital restrictions, especially policies in response to shocks during the financial crisis.

Author details

Aloui Mouna[1*] and Jarboui Anis[2]

1 Department of Financial and Accounting, University of Faculty Economics and Management of Sfax, Tunisia

2 Department of Financial and Accounting, Universities Higher Institute of Business Administration of Sfax, Tunisia

*Address all correspondence to: mounafba@yahoo.fr

References

[1] Charreaux G. Corporate governance théories: From micro théories to national systems théories. Centre de recherche en finance, architecture et gouvernance des organisations, décembre; 2004. pp. 1-57

[2] Beltratti A, Stulz RM. The credit crisis around the globe: Why did some banks perform better? Unpublished working paper. New York, NY: New York University; 2011

[3] Bernanke B. Lessons of the financial crisis for banking supervision. In: Speech presented to Chicago conference on bank structure and competition; 2009. Available from: http://www.federalreserve.gov/newsevents/speech/bernanke20090507a.htm

[4] Kirkpatrick G. The corporate governance lessons from the financial crisis. OECD Journal: Financial Market Trends. 2009

[5] Turnbull S, Pirson M. The future of corporate governance: Network governance—A lesson from the financial crisis. 2010

[6] Bebchuk L, Cohen A, Ferrell A. What matters in corporate governance? Review of Financial Studies. 2009;**22**(2):783-827

[7] Sraer D, Thesmar D. Performance and behavior of family firms: Evidence from the French stock market. Journal of the European Economic Association. 2007;**5**:709-751

[8] Faccio M, Lang L. The separation of ownership and control: An analysis of ultimate ownership in western European corporations. Journal of Financial Economics. 2002;**65**:365-395

[9] Johnson RA, Greening DW. The effects of corporate governance and institutional ownership types on corporate social performance. Academy of Management Journal. 1999;**42**:564-576

[10] La Porta R, Lopez-De-Silanes F, Shleifer A. Corporate ownership around the world. The Journal of Finance. 1999;**542**:471-517

[11] Walker review secretariat. http://webarchive.nationalarchives.gov.uk/+/http:/www.hmtreasury.gov.uk/d/walker_review_261109.pdf

[12] Minton BA, Taillard J, Williamson R. Do independence and financial expertise of the board matter for risk taking and performance? Fisher College of Business Working Paper. (2010-03); 2011. pp. 014

[13] Lemmon M, Lins K. Ownership structure, corporate governance, and firm value: Evidence from the east Asian financial crisis. Journal of Finance. 2003;**58**:1445-1468

[14] Baek JS, Kang JK, Park KS. Corporate governance and firm value: Evidence from the Korean financial crisis. Journal of Financial Economics. 2004;**71**(2):265-313

[15] Huson M, Parrino R, Starks L. Internal monitoring mechanisms and CEO turnover: A long-term perspective. Journal of Finance. 2001;**56**:2265-2297

[16] Choi JJ, Park SE, Yoo SS. The outside directors in Korea: Evidence from corporate governance reform in Korea. Journal of Financial and Quantitative Analysis. 2007;**42**(4):941-962. DOI: 10.1017/S0022109000003458

[17] Huang HH, Chan ML, Huang IH, Chang CH. Stock price volatility and overreaction in a political crisis: The effects of corporate governance and

performance. Pacific-Basin Finance Journal. 2011;**19**(1):1-20

[18] Burcu N, Utku S, S. Serap Y, Yildiz O. The effect of ownership structure on stock prices during crisis periods. International Journal of Business and Social Science. 2012

[19] Jordon SJ, Lee J-H, Bui EA. Outside directors and stock return volatility: The foreign investor connection. 2012. Electronic copy Available from: http://ssrn.com/abstract=2180360

[20] Karolyi GA. A multivariate GARCH model of international transmissions of stock returns and volatility: The case of the United States and Canada. Journal of Business and Economic Statistics. 1995; **13**:11-25

[21] Antoniou A, Holmes P. Futures trading, information and spot price volatility: Evidence for the FTSE-100 stock index futures contract using GARCH. Journal of Banking & Finance. 1995;**19**(1):117-129

[22] Antoniou A, Holmes P, Priestley R. The effects of stock index futures trading on stock index volatility: An analysis of the asymmetric response of volatility to news. Journal of Futures Markets. 1998;**18**(2):151-166

[23] Borokhovich KA, Brunarski KR, Crutchley CE, Simkins BJ. Board composition and corporate use of interest rate derivatives. Journal of Financial Research. 2004;**27**(2): 199-216

[24] Kryvko A APR, Reichling P. Corporate governance and performance of European commercial banks. In: International Conference Improving Financial Institutions: The Proper Balance Between Regulation and Governance; April 2012

[25] Anderson RC, Reeb DM. Board composition: Balancing family influence in S&P 500 firms. Administrative Science Quarterly. 2004;**49**(2):209-237

[26] Pathan S. Strong boards, CEO power and bank risk-taking. Journal of Banking & Finance. 2009;**33**(7): 1340-1350

[27] Wei H, Tao Z. Foreign institutional investors and corporate governance in emerging markets: Evidence of a split-share structure reform in China. Journal of Corporate Finance. 2014;**32**:312-326

[28] Blundell R, Bond S. Initial conditions and moment restrictions in dynamic panel data models. Journal of Econometrics. 1998;**87**:115-143

[29] Vo XV. Foreign ownership and stock return volatility—Evidence from Vietnam. Journal of Multinational Financial Management. 2015;**30**:101-109

[30] Arellano M, Bover O. Another look at the instrumental variable estimation of error-components models. Journal of Econometrics. 1995;**68**:29-52

[31] Longin F, Solnik B. Is the correlation in international equity returns constant: 1960–1990? Journal of International Money and Finance. 1995;**14**(1):3-26

[32] Koulakiotis A, Kartalis N, Lyroudi K, Papasyriopoulos N. The impact of corporate governance, regulatory differences and futures contracts on movements among portfolios of cross-listed equities: The case of Germany. Journal of Multinational Financial Management. 2013;**23**(1):34-53

[33] Zhian C, Jinmin D, Li D, Rui O. Does foreign institutional ownership increase return volatility? Evidence from China. Journal of Banking & Finance. 2013;**3**:660-669

[34] Daily CM, Dalton DR. CEO and board chair roles held jointly or separately: Much ado about nothing?

The Academy of Management Executive. 1997;**11**(3):11-20

[35] Pound J. Proxy contests and the efficiency of shareholder oversight. Journal of Financial Economics. 1988; **20**:237-265

[36] Brickley JA, Lease RC, Smith CW. Ownership structure and voting on antitakeover amendments. Journal of Financial Economics. 1988;**20**:267-291

[37] Agrawal A, Jaffe JF, Mandelker GN. The post-merger performance of acquiring firms: A re-examination of an anomaly. The Journal of Finance. 1992; **47**(4):1605-1621

[38] Cornett MM, Marcus AJ, Saunders A, Tehranian H. The impact of institutional ownership on corporate operating performance. Journal of Banking & Finance. 2007;**31**(6): 1771-1794

[39] Sias R, Starks L, Titman S. Changes in institutional ownership and stock returns: Assessment and methodology. Journal of Business. 2006;**79**:869-910

[40] Dennis PJ, Strickland D. Who blinks in volatile markets, individuals or institutions? The Journal of Finance. 2002;**57**(5):1923-1949

[41] Baber A, Brandt MW, Cosemans M, FM. Ownership Crowded with Style: Institutional Investors, Liquidity, and Liquidity Risk. Last revised November 2012

Section 3

Great Recession Sources

Chapter 3

Source of the Great Recession

Ryo Hasumi, Hirokuni Iiboshi, Tatsuyoshi Matsumae and Shin-Ichi Nishiyama

Abstract

We incorporate two structural shocks associated with balance sheets of both the financial and nonfinancial firms in a medium scale New Keynesian dynamic stochastic general equilibrium (DSGE) model. The structural shocks in the model are assumed to possess stochastic volatilities with a leverage effect. Then, we estimated the model using a data-rich estimation method and utilized up to 40 macroeconomic time series. We found the following three pieces of empirical evidence in the Great Recession (Dec. 2007–Jun. 2009) worsened further by the collapse of Lehman Brothers in September 2008. First, the net-worth shock of financial firms had gradually declined prior to a huge decrease of net-worth of nonfinancial firms. Second, the net worth shock of nonfinancial firms accounted for large weight of the business cycles after the Great Recession, in terms of the data-rich approach with the SV of structural shocks, unlike the standard DSGE model. Third, the Troubled Asset Relief Program would have immediately worked to improve balance sheets of financial institutions, although it would not have stopped worsening those of the corporate sector for a while.

Keywords: new Keynesian model, DSGE model, data-rich approach, Bayesian estimation, financial friction, stochastic volatility, net-worth shock

1. Introduction

The Great Recession (Dec. 2007–Jun. 2009) is thought to have deeply worsened by simultaneous collapse of several big financial institutions besides many bankrupts of the corporate firms and households in the US economy. Recently, a couple of survey papers researching causes of the Great Recession by prominent economists (i.e., Gertler and Gilchrist [1], Kehoe et al. [2]) are published in terms of macroeconomic models, say dynamic stochastic general equilibrium (DSGE) models. Since we obtained a broad consensus that solvency and liquidity problems of the financial institutions are chief among the fundamental factors causing the recession itself, as described in above papers, it is plausible to incorporate financial frictions in both the banking and the corporate sectors of a New Keynesian (NK) DSGE model in order to analyze the recession. Meanwhile, Mian and Sufi [3] analyzed the Great Recession from the aspect of household balance sheets and employment.

The purpose of this study is to identify what structural exogenous shocks contributed to the Great Recession by analyzing the mutual relationship among macroeconomic and financial endogenous variables in terms of business cycles from the point of view of a DSGE model. In fact, according to Ireland [4], there are three sets of considerations that are premature for existing DSGE models. First, failures of financial institutions and liquidity drain should be endogenously described with other fundamental macroeconomic variables for producing economic insights. Second, most recessions have been associated with a rise in bankruptcies among banking and corporate sectors alike. And recessions have featured systematic problems in the banking and loan industry. And third, declines in housing prices and problems in the credit markets might have played an independent and causal role in the Great Recession's severity. Our study challenges to struggle with the former two exercises of Ireland [4], by identifying two different unobservable net-worth shocks of both banking and corporate sectors in a medium scale NK-DSGE model, into which two different financial frictions are newly embedded. And, we estimate time-varying volatility of these structural shocks in order to examine rapid changes of uncertainty and risk for financial crisis across financial markets and the economy as a whole.

As advanced econometric tool, we adopt a data-rich environment to estimate a NK DSGE model following Smets and Wouters [5, 6] but adding above two financial frictions for the US economy. The advantage of incorporating a data-rich environment into a NK DSGE model is that we can more robustly identify two different net-worth shocks generated by two financial frictions because of decomposing comovements of model variables and idiosyncrasy of measurement errors from observable variables of big macroeconomic panel dataset. And this advantage is also useful to estimate a time-varying stochastic volatilities (SVs) of the structural shocks including financial shocks in the DSGE model and to estimate contributions of financial frictions on the real economy both during the Great Recession and after it, because this framework allows the structural shocks to relax the specifications thanks to big dataset.

By adopting the data-rich environment and SV shocks, we will consider four alternative cases, based on the number of observation variables (11 vs. 40 observable variables) and the specification of the volatilities of the structural shocks (constant volatility vs. time-varying volatility). By comparing the four cases, we report the following three findings of empirical evidence in the Great Recession: (1) the net-worth shock of financial institution had gradually declined prior to a huge decrease of net-worth of corporate sector. (2) The net worth shock of nonfinancial firms played an important role during the Great Recession and after it, in terms of the data-rich NK DSGE model with the SV of structural shocks, unlike the standard NK DSGE model. (3) The Troubled Asset Relief Program (TARP) would have immediately worked to improve balance sheets of financial institutions, although it would not have stopped worsening those of the corporate sector for a while. These findings suggest that it is effective to strengthen the regulation, supervision and risk management of banks for preventing financial crisis. And they seem to support the Basel III framework developed by the Basel Committee in response to the global financial crisis of 2007–2009.

As describing our estimation results, introducing structural SV shocks to a DSGE model has their credible interval narrower than half of the model with constant volatilities that indicates a realistic assumption of the time-varying structural shocks. And it is plausible that the uncertainty is trivial in ordinary times but it becomes to a huge size at the turning points of recessions.

The chapter is organized as follows. Section 2 illustrates two financial frictions of the New Keynesian model. Section 3 presents the estimation technique and data description. Sections 4 and 5 discuss the estimation results and interpretation of the Great Recession in terms of the New Keynesian model. Section 6 concludes the paper.

2. Model

We adopt the stylized DSGE model, often referred to as the medium-scale New Keynesian (NK) model, following Christiano et al. [7] and Smets and Wouters [5, 6], which focused on the nominal rigidities of price level and wage as well as the quadratic adjustment cost of investment and habit formation of consumption as blue arrows shown in **Figure 1(a)**. In this NK model, it is generally assumed that

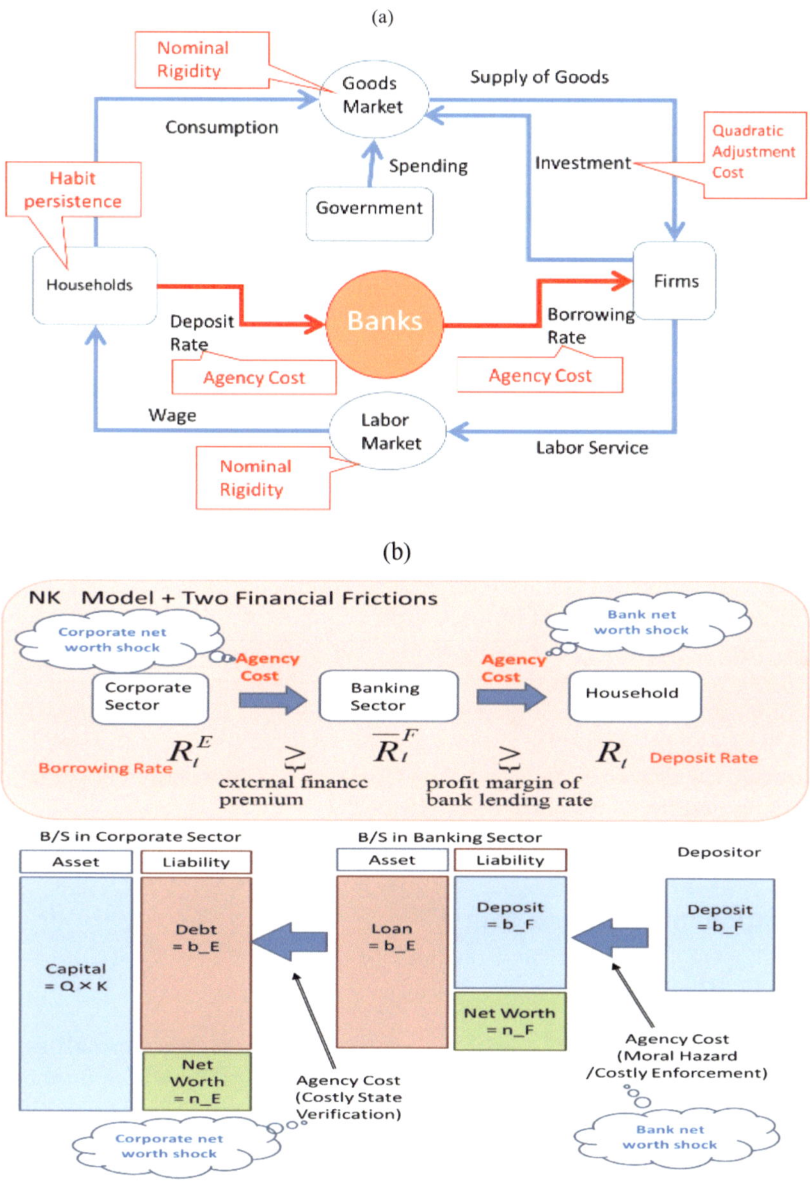

Figure 1.
Our NK model. (a) Flowchart of economy. (b) Two financial frictions. Notes: Panel (a) shows the medium-scale NK model, following Christiano et al. [7] and Smets and Wouters [5, 6], which assume the nominal rigidities of price level and wage as well as the quadratic adjustment cost of investment and habit formation of consumption. Panel (b) shows two financial frictions in which the spread between lending rate R_t^E and deposit rate R_t is divided into two portions by introducing the risk-adjusted return for banks R_t^F in between, and which are modeled to reflect the two different relationship between the balance sheets of the corporate and banking sectors and the borrowers' agency costs against the lenders, respectively.

there are six structural shocks, i.e., (1) preference shock, (2) labor supply shock in households, (3) total factor productivity (TFP) shock, (4) investment-specific technology shock in production function, (5) monetary policy shock and (6) government spending shock in the policy and government sectors.

And, shown as two red arrows in **Figure 1(a)**, we additionally incorporate two different financial frictions in our NK model, since banks have two roles in generating two agency costs with asymmetric information between borrowers and lenders. One is as the lenders to the corporate sector and the other is as the borrowers from depositors. These two financial frictions are designed to reflect the two different relationship between the balance sheets of the corporate and banking sectors and the borrowers' agency costs against the lenders, respectively. The former friction between the bank and the corporate sectors was developed by Bernanke et al. [8], and estimated by Christensen and Dib [9] and Christiano et al. [10]. The latter friction between banks and depositors was proposed by Gertler and Karadi [11] and Gertler and Kiyotaki [12]. Recently, comparisons of both frictions have been studied by Villa [13] and Rannenberg [14] etc. Brumermeier et al. [15] summarized the recent development of these financial friction models of macroeconomics.

In our NK model with the financial frictions, the spread between lending rate R_t^E and deposit rate R_t is divided into two portions by introducing the risk-adjusted return for banks R_t^F in between, as shown in **Figure 1(b)**. The positive corporate net-worth shock shrinks the difference between R_t^E and R_t^F by enlarging the liability of the corporate sector, while the positive bank's net-worth shock shortens the difference between R_t^F and R_t by expanding the liability of the bank sector. Most of DSGE studies adopt independent assumptions of structural shocks, since they are set up originally but not accessional from others and the relaxation of this assumption is involved in difficulty to identify shocks. Following them, it is plausible to assume that these two shocks are independent from one other, since our purpose is to identify different impacts of balance sheet channels of financial and nonfinancial firms on the recessions by measuring sizes of the both financial frictions through the both net-worth shocks of the balance sheets in the these firms.

Decomposing the effects of the two financial frictions on macroeconomic fluctuations might be important for finding out the origin of the Great Recession as well as measuring the degree of damage to the US economy. More detail explanation of this model is described in Iiboshi et al. [16].

3. Estimation methods and data

3.1 Econometric methods

To estimate our NK DSGE model, we adopt two econometric approaches. One is the data-rich approach proposed by Boivin and Giannoni [17], whose method followed by Shorfheide et al. [18], Nishiyama et al. [19] and Iiboshi et al. [20]. The other is to incorporate SV structural shocks in the DSGE model that was proposed by Justiniano and Primiceri [21]. They focused on the Great Moderation using a NK DSGE model with structural shocks with SV framework.

This econometric framework such as the data-rich approach with SV structural shocks can be described as

$$X_t = \Lambda S_t + e_t, \tag{1}$$

$$S_t = \Gamma(\theta) S_{t-1} + \varepsilon_t, \quad \varepsilon_t \sim N\left(0, {\sigma^2}_t\right), \tag{2}$$

$$\log \sigma_t^2 = \mu + \phi \, \log \sigma_{t-1}^2 + \eta_t, \qquad \eta_t \sim N(0,1), \tag{3}$$

where X_t and S_t are vectors of observable and model variables, respectively. ε_t is a vector of structural shocks. σ_t^2 is time-varying variance following autoregressive process such as the third equation, say the SV model. In the framework of the data-rich environment, we make one to many matching relation between S_t and X_t, whereas a standard DSGE model takes one to one matching between them, as shown in **Figure 2**.

3.2 Setting of four cases

Based on above econometric framework, we consider four *alternat*ive cases based on the specification of the volatilities of the structural shocks, σ_t^2, (constant vs. time-varying volatility) and on the number of observation variables, X_t, (11 vs. 40 observable variables) as summarized in **Table 1**. The first case (referred to as **Case A**) dealt with one of the standard DSGE models that used 11 observable variables in the measurement equation and the structural shocks with i.i.d. Normal distribution in the transition equation. The second case (**Case B**) was extended to SV shocks from Case A. The third case (**Case C**) extends to the data-rich approach

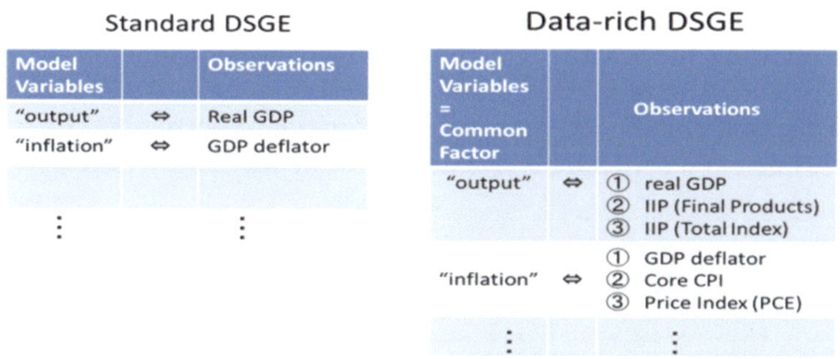

Figure 2.
Data-rich approach. Notes: In the data-rich environment (right panel), we make one to many matching relation between model variables and observations. And in a standard DSGE model (left panel), we take one to one matching relation between them.

	Case A	Case B	Case C	Case D
Types of econometrics framework	Standard DSGE	Standard DSGE	Data-rich DSGE	Data-rich DSGE
Num. of Obs.	**11**	**11**	**40**	**40**
Matching between Model Variables and Obs.	**1 to 1**	**1 to 1**	**1 to 4**	**1 to 4**
Types of Struct. Shocks	iid normal	SV	iid normal	SV

*Notes: The second row denotes types of econometrics framework as shown in **Figure 2**. The third and fourth rows stand for number of observations for estimation and relation between model variables and observations, respectively. The fifth row represents type of distribution of independent structural shocks. Abbreviation "iid" and "SV" denotes identical and independent distribution and stochastic volatilities, respectively.*
For the third row, contents of the observations are described in table of Appendix. 11 observations of Cases A and B are in the first 11 rows of this table, while 40 observations of Cases C and D are all of the table including remains.
For the forth row, "1 to 4" denotes matching one model variables with four observations. A model variable which each observation belongs to is described in the second column of the table.

Table 1.
Setting of four cases.

with i.i.d shocks, including 40 observable variables, which indicate more or less four observable variables corresponding to one specified model variable. And the fourth case (**Case D**) extends to the data-rich approach with SV shocks from Case C.

3.3 Data description

By adopting the data-rich approach, we can adopt a relatively large and quarterly panel dataset with 40 observable variables. (More detail explanation of the observations is in the section, Appendix, in the end of the chapter.) In order to focus on the period of Great Moderation after 1984, we estimate between 1985:Q2 and 2012:Q2 including the Great Recession (Dec. 2007–Jun. 2009) and after it, since avoiding the period of the instable monetary policy regime, especially around the end of the 1970s and the early 1980s, say Hyper Inflation, directed by chairmen of the FRB, P. Volcker and A. Greenspan.

The contents of 40 observations are described in **Appendix** in the end of this chapter. Here, we mention about how to assort them based on the four cases. In Cases A and B, we looked at the following 11 series: (1) output, (2) consumption, (3) investment, (4) inflation, (5) real wage, (6) labor input, (7) the nominal interest rate, (8) the nominal corporate borrowing rate, (9) the external finance premium, (10) the corporate leverage ratio, and (11) the bank leverage ratio. The first seven series are following Smets and Wouters [5, 6]. The four remaining financial observable variables were selected for matching the model variables corresponding to the two financial frictions. The entrepreneur's nominal borrowing rate is the yield on Moody's Baa-rated corporate bonds detrended by the Hodrick-Prescott filter.

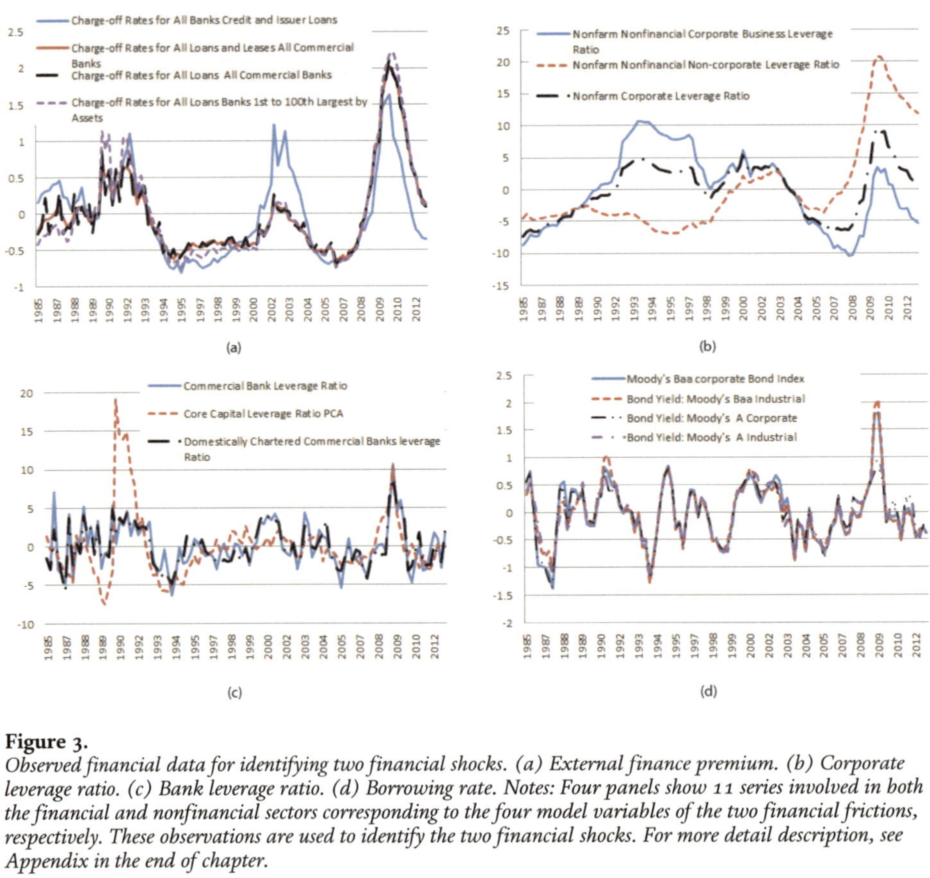

Figure 3.
Observed financial data for identifying two financial shocks. (a) External finance premium. (b) Corporate leverage ratio. (c) Bank leverage ratio. (d) Borrowing rate. Notes: Four panels show 11 series involved in both the financial and nonfinancial sectors corresponding to the four model variables of the two financial frictions, respectively. These observations are used to identify the two financial shocks. For more detail description, see Appendix in the end of chapter.

To measure the external finance premium, we employed the charge-off rates for all banks' credits and issuer loans, measured as an annualized percentage of uncollectible loans. The two leverage ratios were calculated as their total asset divided by their net worth, respectively.

In Cases C and D, to activate the data rich environment, we populate an additional 29 series composed of 18 series of key macroeconomics and 11 series of the banking sector into the existing 11 series in Cases A and B. In **Figure 3(a)**, three different loan charge-off rates based on different institutions are selected as external finance premium. And Panel (c), we take the inverse of the commonly-used ratio, i.e., bank asset over bank equity as the leverage ratio. As shown in this figure, we can find comovements of 11 observations among four kinds of model variables related to the banking sector. In the data rich framework, these comovements are made full use as the model variables, and idiosyncrasy of an observation apart from its comovement is turned out as its measurement error in a DSGE model.

4. Empirical results

Before discussing and remaking the source of Great Recession, we firstly report estimation results, especially focusing on estimations of eight structural shocks by smoothing technique and historical decompositions of four key model variables, (a) output, (b) investment, (c) bank leverage ratio, and (d) borrowing rate, based on the four cases. Those estimations must be significant clue for figuring it out.

4.1 Structural shocks and their volatilities

In Cases A and B estimating standard data structure with the 11 observable variables, the posterior mean (deep blue solid lines) and a 90% credible band (a light blue shade) of the eight structural shocks with constant and time-varying volatilities are drawn in **Figure 4(a)** and **(b)**, respectively. And, **Figure 5(a)** and **(b)** show those of the data rich structure with the 40 observable variables, say Cases C and D, respectively. By comparing estimations of the eight structural shocks of different cases, we observe the following two points. First, although a couple of estimated shocks such as TFP and monetary policy shocks looks very similar among four cases, others, especially labor supply and government spending shocks, have different shapes among the four cases despite using the same DSGE model. Second, every structural shocks with stochastic volatilities (Case B and D) become more volatile in recessions, i.e., 1990:Q2 through 91:Q1, 2001:Q2 through 01:Q3, 2007:Q4 through 08:Q2, and more stable in remaining periods than their counterparts (Case A and C), without regard to data structure used.

Next we consider about financial and nonfinancial net-worth shocks affected on balance sheets on both sectors as shown in the second and third row of **Figures 4** and 5, respectively. Firstly, we can see deep trough at 2008:Q3 in the banking net-worth shocks (the third row) of all cases in these fours figures. In fact, in September and October 2008, major financial institutions such as Lehman Brothers, Merrill Lynch, Fannie Mae, Freddie Mac, Washington Mutual, Wachovia, Citi group, and AIG either failed, were acquired under duress, or were subject to government takeover. On the other hand, the huge troughs of the corporate net-worth shock might not coincide in all cases, and seem to split to two different periods, 2009:Q1 in constant volatility cases (Cases A and C), and 2009:Q2 in stochastic volatilities cases (Cases B and D). However it is worthy of notice that in every case, the corporate net-worth shocks have arrived at deep troughs after the banking sector shocks have experienced its huge drop.

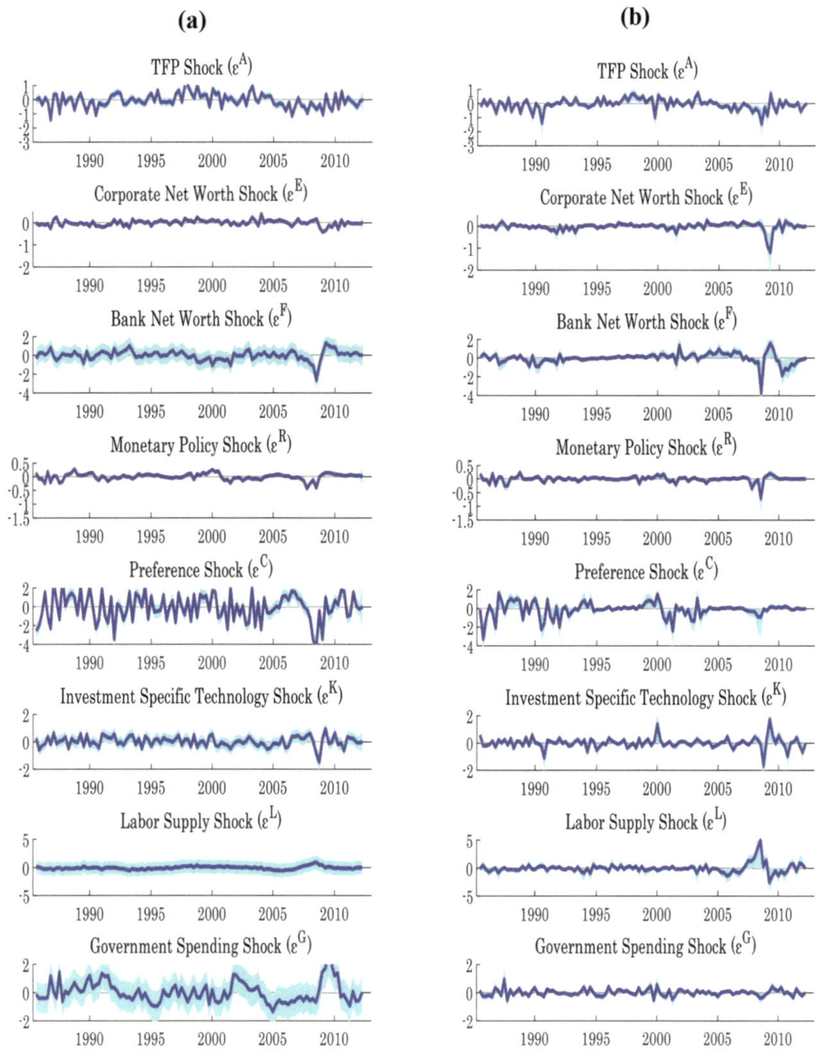

Figure 4.
Structural shocks of standard data structure. (a) Constant volatility: Case A. (b) Stochastic volatility: Case B. Notes: Case A and Case B are described in ***Table 1****. Eight shocks in our DSGE model are explained in Section 2. Corporate Net Worth shock and Bank Net Worth are balance sheet shocks of nonfinancial and financial sectors described in* ***Figure 1(b)****. TFP (total factor productivity), investment specific technology, and labor shock are belong to supply shocks, whereas preference of consumers, monetary policy, and government spending shocks belong to demand shocks. The deep blue lines and blue shaded area are posterior mean and 90% credible interval of structural shocks in Cases A and B, respectively.*

In order to measure the accuracy of the eight estimated shocks, we calculate an average range of 90% credible interval across all of the sample period as **Figures 4** and 5. When the average of 90% interval of a shock of one case become smaller than those of another case, then we can regard that the shock of the case is more precisely identified than another case. Although we leave out the explanation of detail values, averages of five shocks, say (1) preference, (2) banking net worth, (3) labor supply, (4) government spending, and (5) monetary policy, are less in stochastic volatilities cases, B and D, than constant volatilities cases, A and C. In Cases B and D, the averages in the former three shocks are around half against those in Cases A and C. Furthermore, average of government spending shocks downscales by one eighth to one tenth. From these results, we infer that the time-varying volatilities of shocks might be more fit to data generation process which we cannot

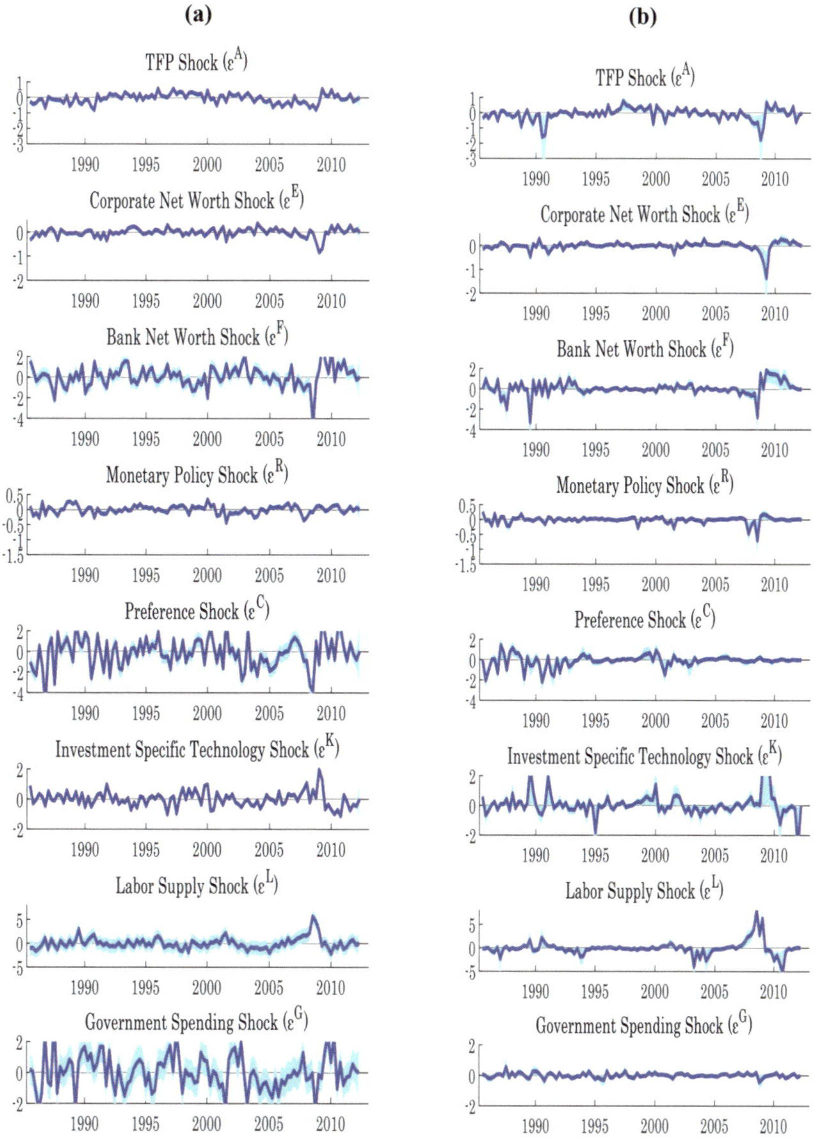

Figure 5.
Structural shocks of data rich environment. (a) Constant volatility: Case C. (b) Stochastic volatility: Case D. Notes: Case C and Case D are described in ***Table 1****. Eight shocks in our DSGE model are explained in Section 2. Corporate Net Worth shock and Bank Net Worth are balance sheet shocks of nonfinancial and financial sectors described in* ***Figure 1(b)****. TFP (total factor productivity), investment specific technology, and labor shock are belong to supply shocks, whereas preference of consumers, monetary policy, and government spending shocks belong to demand shocks. The deep blue lines and blue shaded area are posterior mean and 90% credible interval of structural shocks in Case C and D.*

observe. In addition, we expect that the SV shocks are likely to match for a rapid change of uncertainty and volatilities at the turning points of the Great Recession, rather than the constant volatilities cases, as shown later.

Figure 6 shows the posterior means (deep blue lines) and 90% interval (light blue shade area) of the SVs of all eight shocks for standard data structure (Cases B) and data rich structure (Case D), as well as the posterior means of constant volatilities of the shocks (red dashed flat lines) in Case A and C. As these graphs, in ordinary period, say before the recession, a large part of the deep blue lines (Cases B and D) is under the red dashed lines (Cases A and C). Smoothing SVs of the six

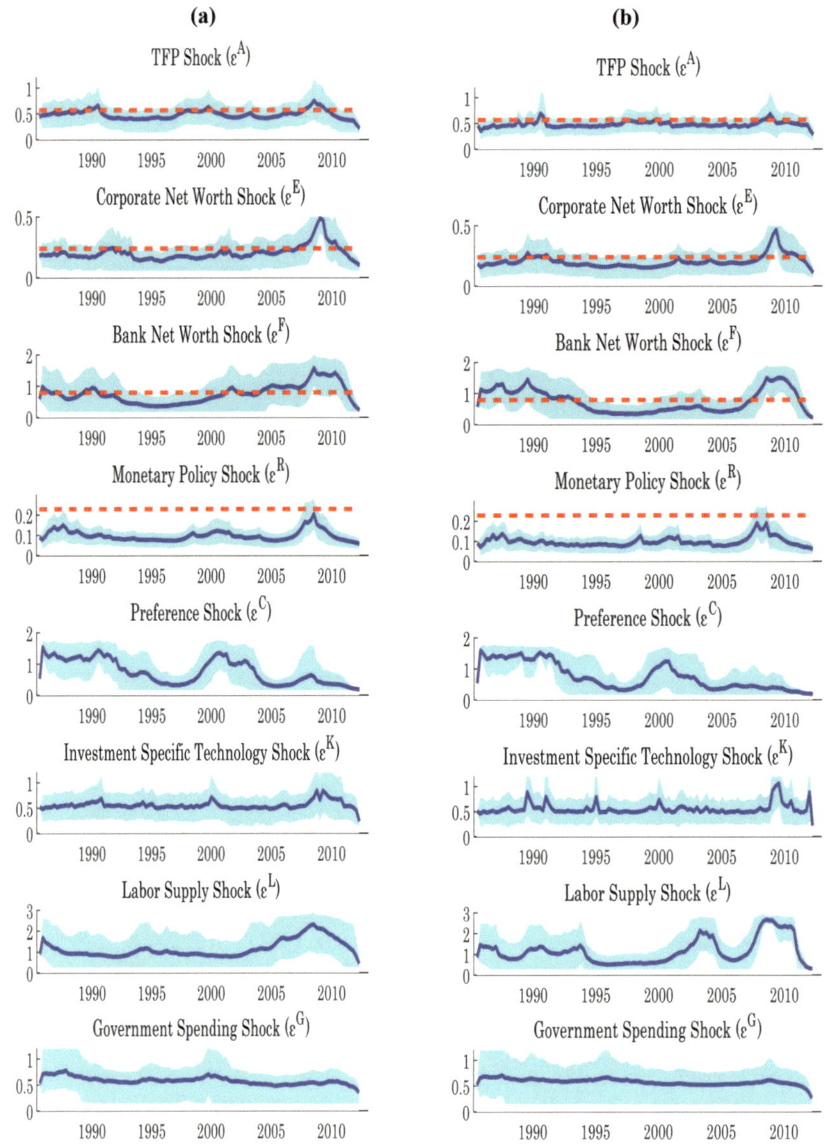

Figure 6.
Stochastic volatilities of structural shocks. (a) Stochastic volatility: Case B. (b) Stochastic volatility data rich: Case D. Notes: Case B and Case D are described in ***Table 1****. Eight shocks in our DSGE model are explained in Section 2. Corporate Net Worth shock and Bank Net Worth are balance sheet shocks of nonfinancial and financial sectors described in* ***Figure 1(b)****. TFP (total factor productivity), investment specific technology, and labor shock are belong to supply shocks, whereas preference of consumers, monetary policy, and government spending shocks belong to demand shocks. The deep blue lines and blue shaded area are posterior mean and 90% credible interval of stochastic volatility (SV) of Cases B and D, respectively. The red dashed lines denote the posterior means of constant volatilities shocks estimated in Case A and C, respectively. SV shocks are explained in Section 3.*

shocks, but investment-specific technology (IST) shock and the labor supply shocks, look very similar in Cases B and D. And the SVs of the preference and labor supply shocks fluctuate with large amplitude during the period of the expansion between 2001:Q4 and 2007:Q4, and it indicates that they have played an important role of boom. Meanwhile, the SVs of the remaining shocks seem to be quiet and level off between 1990:Q1 and 2007:Q3. After August 2007, when the Great Recession began with the seizure in the banking system (in fact, BNP Paribas precipitated ceasing investment activity and was followed by three big hedge funds that

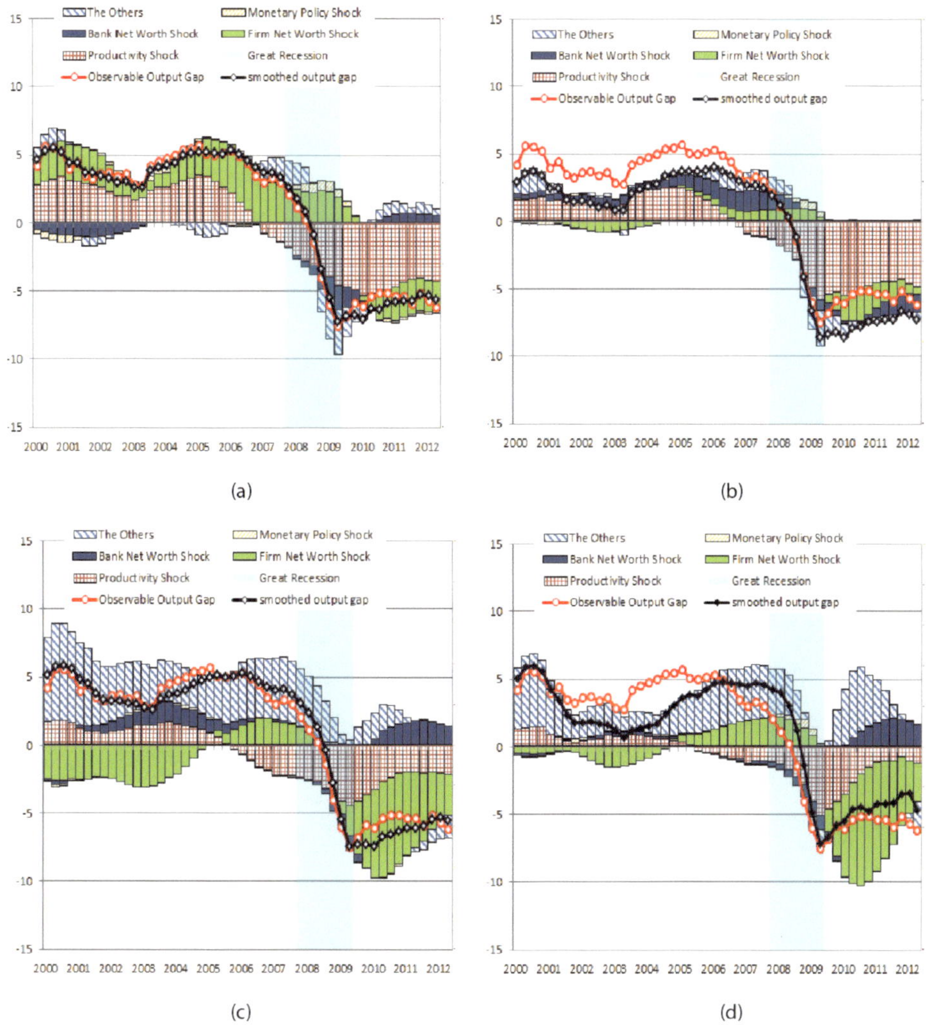

Figure 7.
*Historical decomposition of output. (a) Constant volatility Case A. (b) Stochastic volatility Case B. (c) Constant volatility data rich Case C. (d) Stochastic volatility data rich Case D. Notes: Four Cases A, B, C and D are described in **Table 1**. Case A; 11 observable variables and constant volatility shocks. Case B: 11 observable variables and structural shocks with SV. Case C: 40 observable variables and constant volatility shocks. Case D: 40 observable variables and structural shocks with SVs. Eight shocks are explained in Section 2 and SV shocks are explained in Section 3.*

specialized in US mortgage debt at this moment.), the SVs of net-worth shocks of financial and nonfinancial sectors have rapidly jumped to ceil for both of Case B and D, as well as other shocks such as TFP, monetary policy, IST and labor supply shocks. And levels of these SVs (deep blue lines) exceed the red dashed flat lines indicating estimation of constant volatilities as **Figure 6**.

In this study, we would like to verify whether the data-rich approach contributes to the accuracy of the estimated SVs, compared with standard data structure. **Figures 4(b)** and **5(b)** show averages of the 90% interval (light shade area) in Cases B does not look different from those of Case D. And, although **Figure 6** reports difference in sizes of the 90% intervals (light shade area) of the SVs over the entire sample period between Cases B and D, we do not find obvious improvement of 90% band by the data-rich approach in Case D. From only the three figures, we cannot yet include the data-rich environment improve the accuracy of the SVs estimates. This inquiry will be remained until further research.

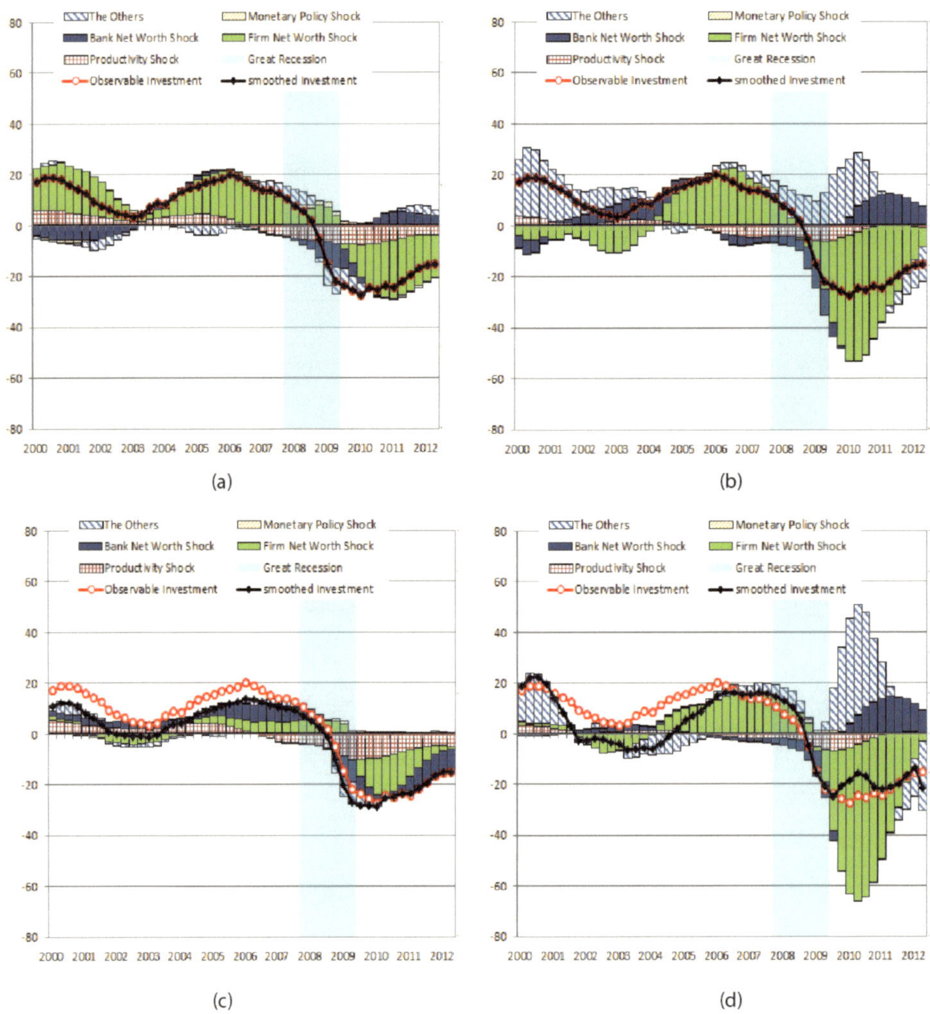

Figure 8.
*Historical decomposition of investment. (a) Constant volatility Case A. (b) Stochastic volatility Case B. (c) Constant volatility data rich Case C. (d) Stochastic volatility data rich Case D. Notes: See the notes of **Figure** 7.*

Finally, we turn to analyzing the monetary policy in the Great Recession and after it including an unconventional monetary policy by FRB such as Round 1 of quantitative easing policy (QE1), between 2008:Q4 and 2010:Q2 and Round 2 of quantitative easing policy (QE2) between 2010:Q4 and 2011:Q2, although our monetary policy rule follows linearized Taylor rules. As the fourth row of **Figures 4** and **5**, we can find the estimation of monetary policy shocks (deep blue lines) have two big negative troughs in this period for all cases. The first negative trough was identified at 2007:Q4 when the global financial market was disarranged by announcement of the BNP Paribas. And the second trough was ascertained at 2008:Q3, immediately before the FRB implemented QE1. Especially, the sizes of the two big negative shocks are classified in the Cases B and D with SVs shocks, as shown in **Figures 4(b)** and **5(b)**. The fourth row of **Figure 6** also draws the rapid surge of these volatilities of monetary policy shocks between 2007:Q4 and 2008:Q3. In other words, the two unconventional monetary policy might be undertaken more boldly and without hesitation as well as the case of conventional tightening policy according to the 90% credible band of the SVs.

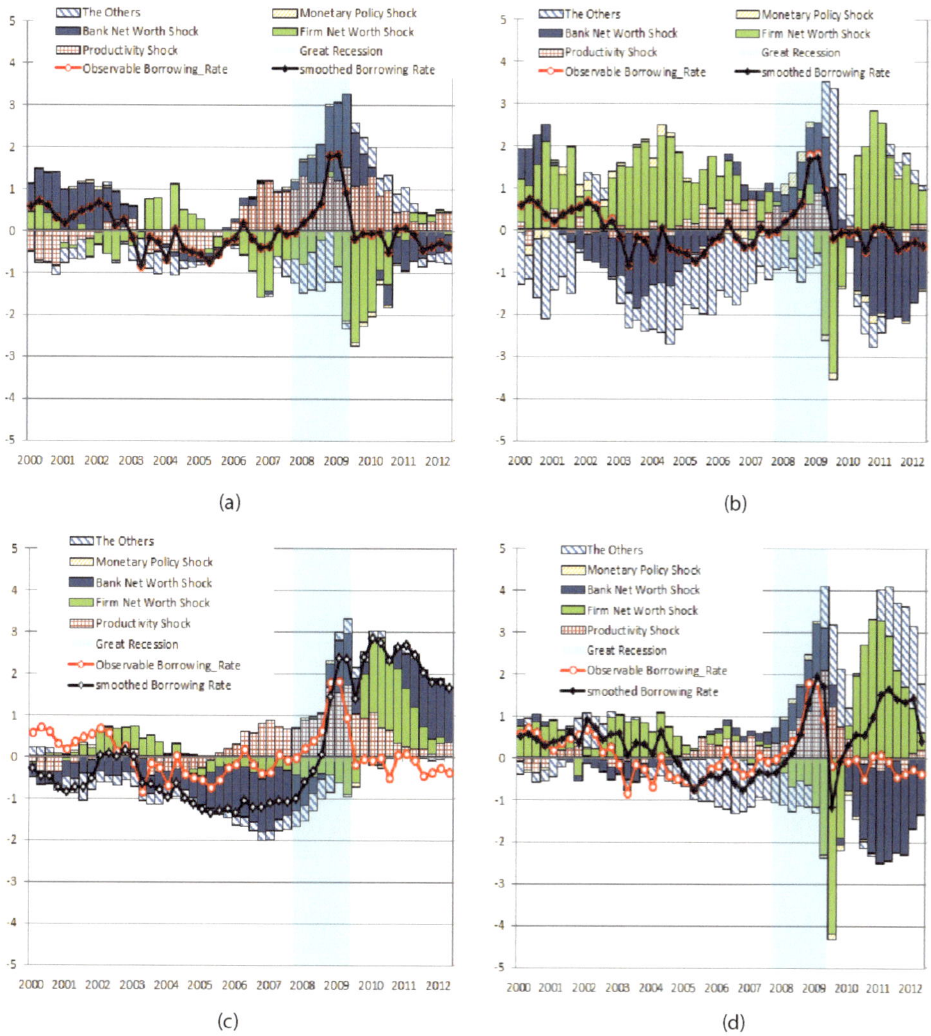

Figure 9.
*Historical decomposition of borrowing rate. (a) Constant volatility Case A. (b) Stochastic volatility Case B. (c) Constant volatility data rich Case C. (d) Stochastic volatility data rich Case D. Notes: See the notes of **Figure 7**.*

4.2 Historical decompositions

Here, we move to discuss about difference of historical decompositions among the four cases. In particular, as can be seen from Figures 7(**a**)–(**d**)–10(**a**)–(**d**), we focus on the periods between 2000:Q1 and 2012:Q2 of the following four observations and model variables, say (1) the real GDP of observations matching to an output gap of model variable, similarly (2) the gross private domestic investment matching to investment, (3) Moody's bond index (corporate Baa) matching to corporate borrowing rate, (4) the commercial banks' leverage ratio matching to the bank leverage ratio. The red and black circle lines represent observations and smoothed estimation, respectively. The differences between both lines indicate measurement errors of observations. In these figures, the light blue shade represents the period of the Great Recession (2007:Q3 to 2009:Q2). In order to make more visible and to concentrate on the contributions of both net-worth shocks of banking sector (deep blue shade area) and corporate sector (green shade area) for the recession by remaining key shocks like the TFP (red shade area) and monetary policy shocks (yellow shade area), we gathered the other four miscellaneous shocks as one bundle (light blue shade area) in these figures.

We start to discuss about real activities, say the real GDP and the gross private domestic investment. As shown in **Figures** 7 and **8**, the contributions by each shocks show similar proportions between the real GDP and the investment. The decomposition by each shock has the same sign at every period of both variables in all four cases, but the sizes of the contribution of shocks are quite different depending on the cases. For example, the TFP shock (red shade area) accounted for a large portion of the sources of the Great Recession, whereas the bank net-worth (deep blue shade area) explained a small part of drops in Cases A and B. And the positive corporate net-worth (green shade area) increased and contributed to raising these variables by a significant portion during the recession in Case A. Meanwhile, Cases C and D showed that the positive impact by the corporate net-worth shock (green shade area) was smaller than Case A, and that the bank net-worth shock (deep blue shade area) explain a half of the downturn of both variables in the recession as well as the TFP shock.

Figure 9 draws historical decomposition of a model variable of corporate borrowing rate using an observation of Moody's bond index (corporate Baa). For all

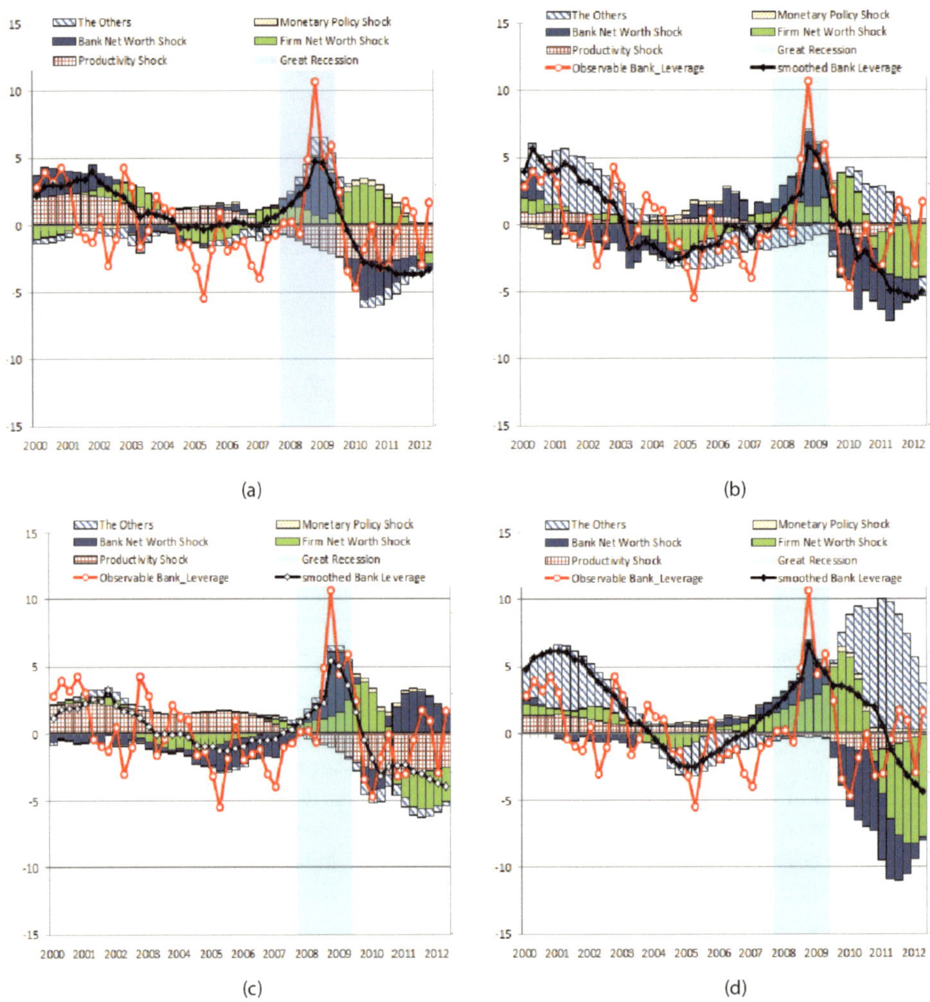

Figure 10.
Historical decomposition of bank leverage ratio. (a) Constant volatility Case A. (b) Stochastic volatility Case B. (c) Constant Volatility Data Rich Case C. (d) Stochastic Volatility Data Rich Case D. Notes: See the notes of ***Figure** 7.*

cases, a sharp spike of the rate must be mainly contributed for the negative shock of bank net-worth (deep blue shade area) as well as from a drop of the TFP shock (red shade area), while the positive shock of corporate net-worth (green shade area) are likely to account for extending of the rate downward in the recession. On the other hand, TARP might have been effectively workable and made the net-worth of financial firms become positive, that would have contributed to decline of the borrowing rate after 2010:Q1. Especially, these findings are seen in Cases B and D with SV shock.

Figure 10 shows the decomposition of the commercial banks' leverage ratio, i.e., the ratio of the bank's asset to the bank's net-worth for all four cases. The leverage ratio fluctuates countercyclical as these figures. In the recession, two negative net-worth shocks of both sectors worsen balance sheet of banking sectors indicating sharp spike of the ratio. But, immediately after starting TARP, bank equity was likely to successfully improve, although the net-worth shock in corporate sector (green shade area) continued negatively and made the corporate balance sheet much worse even during executing TARP in 2010. And the banking loan to corporate sector declined sharply by large deficit of corporate balance sheet. A reduction of banking loan would have brought the banks' leverage ratio to decrease during implement of TARP, because the numerator of the ratio means total of loan and equity in the banks. In fact, we often observe that banking loan declines but corporate bond increases in the recession. However, the countercyclical movement of the bank's leverage ratio was not generated from the banking model by Gertler and Kiyotaki [12] which is one of our financial frictions of banking sector. On the other hand, Adrian et al. [22] intended to describe the reason why the ratio was countercyclical, using a theory of liquidity and leverage proposed by Adrian and Shin [23]. Our findings about two conflicting net-worth shocks in the recession seem to be consistent with Adrian et al.'s [22] findings.

5. Discussion and remark

Through estimation of our model, we found three key findings during the period of the Great Recession and after it, which has already described in the previous section. Without hesitating duplication, we summarize these points.

First, as can be seen from **Figures 4** and **5**, the timing of the two different financial shocks modeling as balance sheet shocks in financial and nonfinancial firms have not arisen simultaneously, but the bank's balance sheet shock has sharply rose prior to the surge of the corporate balance sheet shock. When a financial crisis brings blooming degeneration of both balance sheet, this timing pattern (not concurrent, but sequential timing) must be noted as a lead of endogenous relationship of the balance sheet conditions in both banking sector and the corporate sector. Our model, however, has limitations. That is, we assume the two balance sheet shocks to be independent from each other and further do not allow the corporate sector to keep the bank's equity as an asset of his balance sheet. Thus, it may be inappropriate to interpret the endogenous relationship between the two net-worth shocks. Yet, it is worth noting about remark of the timing pattern of the two financial shocks during the Great Recession.

Second, we found that during the Great Recession, contributions of corporate balance sheet shock are relatively smaller in models with constant volatility shocks as Cases A and C than in models with SV shocks as Cases B and D as shown in **Figures 7–10**. This result suggests that estimation without the data-rich environment is likely to under-evaluate importance of the corporate balance sheet shock. Furthermore, an accuracy of estimating the corporate balance sheet shocks during the Great Recession play an important role of accounting for the economic recovery of the U.S. economy. For instance, in cases with constant volatility shocks as Cases A and C, a slow recovery of output is mainly explained by the negative TFP shock. On the other hand, in cases with SV shocks as Cases B and D, it is mainly explained by a prolonged negative corporate balance sheet shock. The slow recovery of the U.S. economy after the Great Recession remains as an important question, and a persuasive description of this question requests a precise estimation of trace of these shocks. To this end, especially for estimating the corporate net worth shock, we hope that a data-rich approach with SV shocks must be more reliable than standard data structure.

Third, there is another important finding from the historical decomposition which is the behavior of the bank's balance sheet shock. A sharp decline of the bank's balance sheet shock was obviously associated with the Great Recession, and rapid reductions of output and investment have stem from two net-worth shocks, as shown in **Figures** 7 and **8**. Immediately after end of the Great Recession, the bank's balance sheet shock, however, quickly reversed its direction from negative to positive, and picked up both of output and investment upward. When we consider the timing of this reversal, it was plausible that the execution of the TARP is behind this counterturn. That is, TARP would have successfully made downward trend of the bank's balance sheet change upward. From our finding about the positive contribution of the bank's net-worth shock to the real GDP and investment right after the end of the Great Recession period, the executing TARP might be one of the major factors behind the stopping further degeneration of the recession and contributing to the recovery of the U.S. economy.

These three findings seem to support the Basel III framework developed by the Basel Committee in response to the global financial crisis of 2007–2009. The Basel III revised in order to strengthen the regulation, supervision and risk management of banks, by reducing excessive variability of risk-weighted assets (RWA) of banks. In particular, for preventing global financial crisis, it might be effective to restore credibility of the RWA by complementing the risk-weighted capital ratio with a finalized leverage ratio and a revised and robust capital floor, according to our empirical findings.

6. Conclusion

This study is to identify what structural exogenous shocks contributed to the Great Recession and to analyze the mutual relationship among macroeconomic and financial endogenous variables in terms of a medium scale New Keynesian DSGE model with two net-worth shocks in both the financial and nonfinancial firms, using data rich approach with as many as 40 observations. And it is plausible to incorporate two different financial frictions to a standard DSGE model to analyze the recession, since there was a broad consensus that solvency and liquidity problems of the major financial institutions such as Lehman Brothers, Merrill Lynch, Fannie Mae, Freddie Mac, Washington Mutual, Wachovia, Citi group, and AIG, which either failed, were acquired under duress, or were subject to government takeover, might be attributed causing the Great Recession itself.

We considered four alternative cases based on the number of observation variables (11 vs. 40 variables) and the specification of the volatilities of the structural shocks (constant volatility vs. time-varying-volatility). Comparing these four cases, we suggested the following two pieces of empirical evidence in the Great Recession; (1) the negative bank net worth shock gradually spread before the corporate net worth shock burst, and (2) the data-rich approach and the structural shocks with SV evaluated the contribution of the corporate net worth shock to a substantial portion of the macroeconomic fluctuations after the Great Recession, in contrast to a standard DSGE model.

From a view of evaluating policies, the implementation of TARP has sufficiently worked to mitigate the bank's negative net-worth shocks und upturned the output and the investment. The model and empirical results in this study suggest that such a bail-out program must be workable effectively in case of a serious recession followed by a financial crisis with failures of financial institutions. On the other hand, the slow recovery of the U.S. economy after the Great Recession can be explained by the wounded balance sheet of the non-financial corporate sector, which is not healed in a short period.

Acknowledgements

The authors would like to especially appreciate Micheal Julliard (Bank of France) and Rafael Wouters (National Bank of Belgium) for their comments. And they also thank discussion with Gianni Amisano, Ryo Jinnai, Tatsuyoshi Okimoto, Tsutomu Miyagawa, Masaya Sakuragawa, Tasturo Senga, Etsuro Shioji, Hajime Tomura, Toshiaki Watanabe and other participants of the seminars at Gakusyuin Univ. and Osaka Univ. and at International Conference of Advanced Macroecononometrics 2013 held at Hitotsubashi Univ., 4th ESRI-CEPREMAP joint workshop 2013, 10th Biennial Pacific Rim Conference by Western Economic Association, 46th annual conference of Money Macro and Finance (MMF) 2014 at Univ. of Durham, the annual meeting of Canadian Economic Association 2014, and Autumn Meeting of Japan Society of Monetary Economics 2018, We also thank kindly comments from Yasuharu Iwata and Koichi Yano in the process of writing the study. Remaining errors should be regarded as those solely of the authors.

Appendix

No.	Variables	Proc.	Observation explanation	Unit of data	Source
Case A and Case B: The standard Data Structure					
1	$\mathbf{R}$	6	Interest rate: Federal Funds Effective Rate	% per annum	FRB
2	$\mathbf{Y_1}$	5	Real gross domestic product (excluding net export)	Billion of chained 2000	BEA
3	$\mathbf{C_1}$	5*	Gross personal consumption expenditures	Billion dollars	BEA
4	$\mathbf{I_1}$	5*	Gross private domestic investment - Fixed investment	Billion dollars	BEA
5	π_1	8	Price deflator: Gross domestic product	2005Q1 = 100	BEA
6	$\mathbf{w_1}$	2	Real Wage (Smets and Wouters, 2007)	1992Q3 = 0	SW (2007)
7	$\mathbf{L_1}$	1	Hours Worked (Smets and Wouters, 2007)	1992Q3 = 0	SW (2007)
8	$\mathbf{RE_1}$	6	Moody's bond indices - corporate Baa	% per annum	Bloomberg
9	$\mathbf{Lev_1^F}$	7	Commercial banks leverage ratio	Total asset/net worth ratio	FRB
10	$\mathbf{Lev_1^E}$	3	Nonfarm non-fin. Corp. business leverage ratio	Total asset/net worth ratio	FRB
11	$\mathbf{s_1}$	1	Charge-off rates for all banks credit and issuer loans	% per annum	FRB

No.	Variables	Proc.	Observation explanation	Unit of data	Source
Case C and Case D: The data-Rich Environment					
12	Y_2	4	Industrial production index: final products	Index 2007 = 100	FRB
13	Y_3	4	Industrial production index: total index	Index 2007 = 100	FRB
14	Y_4	4	Industrial production index: products	Index 2007 = 100	FRB
15	C_2	5*	PCE excluding food and energy	Billions of dollars	BEA
16	C_3	5	Real PCE, quality indexes; non-durable goods	Index 2005 = 100	BEA
17	C_4	5	Real PCE, quality indexes; services	Index 2005 = 100	BEA
18	I_2	5	Real gross private domestic investment	Billions of Chained 2005	BEA
19	I_3	5*	Gross private domestic investment: fixed nonresidential	Billions of dollars	BEA
20	I_4	5	Manufactures' new orders: non-defense capital goods	Millions of dollars	DOC
21	π_2	8	Core CPI excluding food and energy	Index 2005 = 100	BEA
22	π_3	8	Price index - PCE excluding food and energy	Index 2005 = 100	BEA
23	π_4	8	Price index - PCE - Service	Index 2005 = 100	BEA
24	w_2	4*	Average hourly earnings: manufacturing	Dollars	BLS
25	w_3	4*	Average hourly earnings: construction	Dollars	BLS
26	w_4	4*	Average hourly earnings: service	Dollars	BLS
27	L_2	4	Civilian Labor Force: Employed Total	Thous.	BLS
28	L_3	4	Employees, nonfarm: total private	Thous.	BLS
29	L_4	4	Employees, nonfarm: goods-producing	Thous.	BLS
30	RE_2	6	Bond yield: Moody's Baa industrial	% per annum	Bloomberg
31	RE_3	6	Bond yield: Moody's A corporate	% per annum	Bloomberg
32	RE_4	6	Bond yield: Moody's A industrial	% per annum	Bloomberg
33	Lev_2^F	9	Core capital leverage ratio PCA all insured institutions	Core capital/total asset	FDIC
34	Lev_3^F	7	Domestically chartered commercial banks leverage ratio	Total asset/net worth	FRB
35	Lev_4^F	7	Brokers and dealers leverage ratio	Total asset/net worth	FOF
36	Lev_2^E	3	Nonfarm nonfinancial non-corporate leverage ratio	Total asset/net worth	FOF
37	Lev_3^E	3	Nonfarm corporate leverage ratio	Total asset/net worth	FRB
38	s_2	1	Charge-off rate on all loans and leases all commercial banks	% per annum	FRB
39	s_3	1	Charge-off rate on all loans all commercial banks	% per annum	FRB
40	s_4	1	Charge-off rate on all loans banks 1st to 100th largest by assets	% per annum	FRB

Notes: Table is composed from the following five columns, say Number, Model Variable Name, Transformation Procedures, Observation Explanations, Unit of Data, and Data Source. Abbreviations such as "PCE" and "SW (2007)", stand for personal consumption expenditure and Smets and Wouters (2007), respectively. In a column of the Transformation Procedures, numbers stand for 1: Demeaned, 2: Linear and De-trended, 3: Logarithm and Demeaned, 4: Logarithm, Linear De-trended, and Multiplied by 100, 5: Logarithm per Capita, Linear De-trended and Multiplied by 100, 6: De-trended using Hodrick-Prescott (HP) filter, 7: Logarithm, De-trended using HP Filter, and Multiplied by 100, 8: First Difference Logarithm, De-trended using HP Filter, and Multiplied by 400, 9: the Reciprocal number, Logarithm, De-trended using HP Filter, and Multiplied 100.
*A * indicate a series that is deflated with the GDP deflator.*

Author details

Ryo Hasumi[1], Hirokuni Iiboshi[2]*, Tatsuyoshi Matsumae[3] and Shin-Ichi Nishiyama[4]

1 Musashi University, Tokyo, Japan

2 Tokyo Metropolitan University, Tokyo, Japan

3 Tohoku University, Sendai, Japan

4 Kobe University, Kobe, Japan

*Address all correspondence to: iiboshi@tmu.ac.jp

References

[1] Gertler M, Gilchrist S. What happened: Financial factors in the great recession. The Journal of Economic Perspectives. 2018;**32**(3):3-30

[2] Kehoe PJ, Midrigan V, Pastorino E. Evolution of modern business cycle models: Accounting for the great recession. The Journal of Economic Perspectives. 2018;**32**(3): 141-166

[3] Mian A, Sufi A. What explains the 2007-2009 drop in employment? Econometrica. 2014; **82**(6):2197-2223

[4] Ireland PN. A new Keynesian perspective on the great recession. Journal of Money, Credit, and Banking. 2011;**43**(1):31-54

[5] Smets F, Wouters R. An estimated dynamic stochastic general equilibrium model of the euro area. Journal of the European Economic Association. 2003; **1**(5):1123-1175

[6] Smets F, Wouters R. Shocks and frictions in US business cycles: A Bayesian DSGE approach. The American Economic Review. 2007; **97**(3):586-606

[7] Cristiano LJ, Eichenbaum M, Evans C. Nominal rigidities and the dynamic effects of a shock to monetary policy. Journal of Political Economy. 2005;**113**:1-45

[8] Bernanke BS, Gertler M, Gilchrist S. The financial accelerator in a quantitative business cycles framework. In: Taylor JB, Woodford M, editors. Handbook of Macroeconomics. Vol. 1C. Amsterdam, Netherlands: Elsevier; 1999. pp. 1341-1393

[9] Christensen I, Dib A. The financial accelerator in an estimated new Keynesian model. Review of Economic Dynamics. 2008;**11**:155-178

[10] Christiano LJ, Motto R, Rostagno M. Risk Shocks. The American Economic Review. 2014;**104**(1):27-65

[11] Gertler M, Karadi P. A model of unconventional monetary policy. Journal of Monetary Economics. 2011; **58**:17-34

[12] Gertler M, Kiyotaki N. Financial intermediation and credit policy in business cycle analysis. In: Friedman BM, Woodford M, editors. Handbook of Monetary Economics. Vol. 3. Amsterdam, Netherlands: Elsevier; 2010. pp. 547-599

[13] Villa S. Financial friction in the euro area and the United States: A Bayesian assessment. Macroeconomic Dynamics. 2017;**20**(05):1313-1340

[14] Rannenberg A. Bank leverage cycles and the external finance premium. Journal of Money, Credit, and Banking. 2016;**48**(8):1569-1612

[15] Brunnermeier MK, Eisenbach TM, Sannikov Y. Macroeconomics with financial frictions: a survey. NBER Working Paper No. 18102; 2012

[16] Iiboshi H, Matsumae T, Nishiyama S-I. Sources of the Great Recession: A Bayesian Approach of a Data-Rich DSGE model with Time-Varying Volatility Shocks. ESRI Discussion paper series 313, Economic and Social Research Institute; 2014

[17] Boivin J, Giannoni M. DSGE models in a data-rich environment [thesis]. HEC Montreal and Columbia University; 2006

[18] Shorfheide F, Sill K, Kryshko M. DSGE model-based forecasting of

non-modelled variables. International Journal of Forecasting. 2010;**26**:348-373

[19] Nishiyama S.-I, Iiboshi H, Matsumae T, Namba R. How bad was Lehman shock?: Estimating a DSGE model with firm and bank balance sheets in a data-rich environment. Mimeo; 2011

[20] Iiboshi H, Matsumae T, Namba R, Nishiyama S-I. Estimating a DSGE model for Japan in a data-rich environment. Journal of the Japanese and International Economies. 2015;**36**: 25-55

[21] Justiniano A, Primiceri G. The time-varying volatility of macroeconomic fluctuations. The American Economic Review. 2008;**98**(3):604-641

[22] Adrian T, Colla P, Shin HS. Which financial frictions? Parsing the evidence from the financial crisis of 2007-09. NBER Macroeconomics Annual. 2013; **27**(1):159-214

[23] Adrian T, Shin HS. Liquidity and leverage. Journal of Financial Intermediation. 2010;**19**(3):418-437

Section 4

The "Alchemy" behind the Financial Crisis

Chapter 4

Political and Institutional Dynamics of the Global Financial Crisis

Shanuka Senarath

Abstract

Asset securitization has been identified as an alchemy that 'really' works. Asset securitization yields a number of benefits to a financial system inter alia by reducing overall interest rates, enhancing liquidity in the banking sector and reducing intermediary costs. Yet, the recent global financial crisis (GFC) questioned the very existence of asset securitization. However, post-GFC literature is not hesitant to identify a list of causes that may have facilitated the GFC including subprime lending, executive compensation, de-regulation, etc. Adopting a lexonomic approach, this discussion deviates from the traditional approach by focusing on identifying political and institutional factors behind the GFC. This chapter will investigate U.S political economic decision and then U.S institutional setup that may have facilitated the stage for a GFC.

Keywords: asset-securitization, global financial crisis, asset-backed-securities

1. Introduction

This chapter provides a contextual background to those that follow by describing the GFC and its salient characteristics, and identifying salient causes of the crisis. Once these salient causes have been identified, the thesis proceeds to investigate the extent of the role, if any, that economics and political mechanisms underlying securitization may have had in facilitating the GFC. Financial economists generally trace the beginnings of the GFC to approximately mid-2007, when a number of key mortgage lenders specialising in sub-prime housing loans experienced financial distress. For a number of reasons, banks and other mortgage originators had, in the years preceding the GFC, been able to lend home loans to low-to-mid-income borrowers[1] This practice, and the securitization arrangements based on it, would generally not have proved problematic if house prices throughout the United States had continued to appreciate as they had under speculative boom conditions. Problems arose, however, when the U.S. housing boom burst in 2006, and particularly in residential areas housing concentrations of 'sub-prime' borrowers.

---

[1] Often referred as subprime borrowers who, under normal lending criteria, would have been refused loans (eg. because of poor credit histories).

IntechOpen

As investors became increasingly reluctant to invest in securities based on sub-prime housing mortgages, this financial distress spread to securitizers of a sub-prime mortgage loans, and was further exacerbated when credit rating agencies such as Standard & Poor's, Moody's, and Fitch downgraded many mortgage-backed securities. In the words of Allen and Carletti, the mortgage-backed sub-prime home loan securitization market 'simply broke down' [1] and a general loss of confidence became more widespread, affecting commercial asset-backed securitization markets in the latter half of 2007. Banks sponsoring many residential and commercial securitizers were required, under the terms of cross-guarantee arrangements, to pay debts that otherwise would have remained off-balance-sheet as contingent liabilities [2].

Institutional and corporate investors internationally had also purchased securitization products, adding to the linkages between large financial institutions in different jurisdictions. At about the same time, other banks in the United States, Britain and elsewhere in Europe—themselves uncertain about the extent to which they might be called to make unexpectedly large payments from their reserves under their own cross-guarantee arrangements with related securitizers and other companies—became reluctant to provide any more than very short term liquidity (of more than a few days' tenor) to each other. Institutional investors engaged in a 'flight to quality', investing in highly liquid, secure assets such as Treasury bills and other government securities. In approximately March 2008, company reports of further bad debts and asset write-downs because of mark-to-market accounting increased uncertainty about counterparty risk levels, with the result that global investment bank Bear Stearns Companies Inc. was unable to secure wholesale funding to continue its operations past mid-March, when it was sold to JP Morgan Chase & Co. for approximately 7% of its pre-crisis equity value [3].

Internationally, central banks in consultation with their governments intervened in their respective economies by markedly reducing official or cash rates; injecting liquidity into the system by effectively lending to primary dealers (e.g. by allowing them to swap less liquid asset-backed securities for Treasury securities, often at a substantial discount); and so-called government 'bailouts' of securitizing institutions perceived to be economically significant or 'too big to fail' (such as Northern Rock in Britain; and Bear Stearns, Fannie Mae and Freddie Mac in the U.S.) [4, 5].[2] In subsequent months, real economies in the United States, Britain and elsewhere in Europe have exhibited historically poor performance, with relatively high unemployment and low economic growth, despite relatively low interest rates and inflation.

Abstracting somewhat from this background, the GFC's chief characteristics as identified in the literature can be clustered around excessive system liquidity; high levels of executive compensation by community standards; high levels of financial innovation; banks and other financial intermediaries undertaking activities beyond

[2] A number of high-profile investment bank securitizers requested government support, including Bear Stearns, Merrill Lynch, Wachovia, Goldman Sachs, and Morgan Stanley. Of these, Bear Stearns, Merrill Lynch and Wachovia were ultimately sold at well below their year high equity prices, while Goldman Sachs and Morgan Stanley ultimately became commercial bank holding companies, subject to prudential regulation but able to access Federal Reserve swaps into liquid assets at substantially discounted prices. Another high-profile securitizer, Lehman Brothers, went into involuntary liquidation. American International Group (AIG), a global insurer and sub-insurer which had ultimately insured many of the securitization schemes affected by collapsing asset prices, was saved from liquidation by a U.S. Federal Reserve Bank 'rescue package' that enabled AIG to deliver additional collateral to its credit default swap trading partners

their traditional roles; speculative asset bubbles; and the U.S. sub-prime crisis and the fallout resulting from it [6, 7].

This chapter looks into the main causes of the crisis, while developing a discussion on the contribution of each individual factor for the onset of the financial crisis. The chapter finds that GFC 2007 is a result of a number of factors. Some factors are linked with political decisions dated decades back in U.S political agenda, while some factors are market driven. The structure of the chapter is as fallows. Section 2 is a brief discussion on history of financial crisis in the modern world. Section 3, the main section of the chapter is a discussion on GFC 2007, with a special emphasis on housing bubble. This section glances over a number of contributory factors to the GFC including inter alia economical, financial, legal and behavioural factors that may have contributed to the onset of the crisis.

2. Speculative asset bubbles in modern financial history

Although examples of speculative bubbles are recorded in ancient times, in more recent times the most commonly cited early example of a speculative asset bubble is the Tulip Bubble in the 1600s. Tulips imported from East to Holland in the 1600s became a collector's item, and tulip bulbs were sold as very high prices. An influx of speculative funds was accompanied by a surge in financial innovation until the bubble burst in 1673, and many who had purchased bulbs on credit went bankrupt, precipitating an economic depression all over the country [8, 9].

A second commonly cited speculative bubble in early modern financial history was the collapse of the South Sea Company, reported in England in 1720. The South Sea Company was a joint stock company, which was awarded a Royal Charter (monopoly rights) to trade in North and South America, and became the subject of massive speculation throughout Europe. The company's share price, recorded at £128 in January 1720, increased almost tenfold to £1000 over the next 6 months to July 1720. By the end of 1720 following a bursting of the bubble, however, it had reverted to £124 per share [10].

It was in early 1920s that the Florida real estate bubble burst. However the ability to purchase real estate with a down payment of 10% provided the leverage to the asset bubble. Accordingly house prices went up grabbing more peculators in to the business. The bubble burst in advance with a typhoon hitting Florida causing massive property damage. The sudden drop in prices paved the way for bankruptcies and default. The Great depression, the most longest, widespread, and deepest depression of the 20th century took place after the stock market crash of October 29, 1929. The speculative asset bubble started to grow in late 1920s' with the boom in many industries[3] resulting stock market speculation and paving way for thousands of investors to invest in the stock market, were as most of the investors have borrowed the money for investments. The asset bubble rose to such a high extent that the lenders have given loans up to three times of the face value of the stocks investors have purchased. Expecting stock prices to raise more, more and more funds were invested in the stock market creating a massive asset bubble by 1929. At the end with the dropping commodity prices the stock prices began to fall. By October 29, panic selling started and the stock market collapsed, leading to the longest depression in the world history [11–14].

The 'Tronics' burst took place in 1961 with emergence of electronics in the market. A number of investors were keen on investing shares belonging to

[3] Steel production, building, automobiles etc.

companies dealing with electronics. With the bubble burst in 1962, the share prices went down significantly. A speculative asset bubble, similar to the bubble in 1920s, took place in US by 1984. The speculative asset bubble was believed to be built on leverage and loose government economic policy. Similar to the event took place in 1920s. Junk bonds were the financial innovation of the day. The debts of less creditworthy companies were used as a tool to purchasing companies. Program trading and stock index futures were the other financial innovations. The Bubble peaked in October of 1987 followed by a stock market crash in a in a single day. Even though the public expectation was an economic depression, with the federal guarantee that they would guarantee the credit of market makers the recession never took place [15, 16].

In 2007 the housing prices in US believed to have grown more than 100%, within a decade's time. These bubble in house prices paved the way for house owners to refinance their houses at a lower rate and further to gain a second mortgage with backed by the price appreciation. Backed by large investment banks, small banks funded brokers by buying loans for the mortgage broker. Lending to the subprime market was significant by the time, enhancing the housing bubble. Compared to 2006 the housing prices declined 20% by September 2008. Leading borrowers to default. Douglas et al. (2012) identifies the 2007-8 Global financial crisis had resulted in significant negative impact all over the world, while making policy makes re-consider the fact that they can or should manage such asset bubbles [5–7].

Humans never seems to learn from their mistakes as greed becomes the prominent decision making factor for the human-financial decision making.[4] The main factor that distinguish GFC from the rest of the crises is the fact that DFC 2007 is based on a housing bubble. Yet, ironically all financial crises are based on some sort of an asset. In 1600s it was the Tulip Bubble. In South Sea bubble it was company stocks. Again in dot.com bubble it was company stocks. In each occasion a financial asset accumulates its price creating a bubble, which breakouts suddenly with changes in surrounding economic factors. Hence at a glance the GCF is quite unique, since it developed on real estate prices. Yet, a deep analysis revels that underling mechanism of the GFC is no difference to the rest.

3. The global financial crisis (GFC)

Financial economists generally trace the beginnings of the GFC to approximately mid-2007, when a number of key mortgage lenders specialising in sub-prime housing loans experienced financial distress. For a number of reasons set out below, banks and other mortgage originators had, in the years preceding the GFC, been able to lend home loans to low-to-mid-income borrowers who, under normal lending criteria, would have been refused loans (e.g. because of poor credit histories). This practice, and the securitization arrangements based on it, would generally not have proved problematic if house prices throughout the United States had continued to appreciate as they had under speculative boom conditions. Problems arose, however, when the U.S. housing boom burst in 2006, and particularly in residential areas housing concentrations of 'sub-prime' borrowers [5, 6, 17].

[4] See in general the discussion developed based on the concept 'casino capitalism' in Keynes's General theory [18].

As investors became increasingly reluctant to invest in securities based on sub-prime housing mortgages, this financial distress spread to securitizers of a sub-prime mortgage loans, and was further exacerbated when credit rating agencies such as Standard & Poor's, Moody's, and Fitch downgraded many mortgage-backed securities. In the words of Allen and Carletti, the mortgage-backed sub-prime home loan securitization market 'simply broke down' and a general loss of confidence became more widespread, affecting commercial asset-backed securitization markets in the latter half of 2007. Banks sponsoring many residential and commercial securitizers were required, under the terms of cross-guarantee arrangements, to pay debts that otherwise would have remained off-balance-sheet as contingent liabilities [6, 17].

Institutional and corporate investors internationally had also purchased securitization products, adding to the linkages between large financial institutions in different jurisdictions. At about the same time, other banks in the United States, Britain and elsewhere in Europe—themselves uncertain about the extent to which they might be called to make unexpectedly large payments from their reserves under their own cross-guarantee arrangements with related securitizers and other companies—became reluctant to provide any more than very short term liquidity (of more than a few days' tenor) to each other. Institutional investors engaged in a 'flight to quality', investing in highly liquid, secure assets such as Treasury bills and other government securities. In approximately March 2008, company reports of further bad debts and asset write-downs because of mark-to-market accounting increased uncertainty about counterparty risk levels, with the result that global investment bank Bear Stearns Companies Inc. was unable to secure wholesale funding to continue its operations past mid-March, when it was sold to JP Morgan Chase & Co. for approximately 7% of its pre-crisis equity value [2, 19].

Internationally, central banks in consultation with their governments intervened in their respective economies by markedly reducing official or cash rates; injecting liquidity into the system by effectively lending to primary dealers (e.g. by allowing them to swap less liquid asset-backed securities for Treasury securities, often at a substantial discount); and so-called government 'bailouts' of securitizing institutions perceived to be economically significant or 'too big to fail' (such as Northern Rock in Britain; and Bear Stearns, Fannie Mae and Freddie Mac in the U.S.).[5] In subsequent months, real economies in the United States, Britain and elsewhere in Europe have exhibited historically poor performance, with relatively high unemployment and low economic growth, despite relatively low interest rates and inflation [20].

Abstracting somewhat from this background, the GFC's chief characteristics as identified in the literature can be clustered around excessive system liquidity; high levels of executive compensation by community standards; high levels of financial innovation; banks and other financial intermediaries undertaking activities beyond their traditional roles; speculative asset bubbles; and the U.S. sub-prime crisis and the fallout resulting from it.

---

[5] A number of high-profile investment bank securitizers requested government support, including Bear Stearns, Merrill Lynch, Wachovia, Goldman Sachs, and Morgan Stanley. Of these, Bear Stearns, Merrill Lynch and Wachovia were ultimately sold at well below their year high equity prices, while Goldman Sachs and Morgan Stanley ultimately became commercial bank holding companies, subject to prudential regulation but able to access Federal Reserve swaps into liquid assets at substantially discounted prices. Another high-profile securitizer, Lehman Brothers, went into involuntary liquidation [21].

3.1 Law creates incentives

Even though each crisis has some link with the then legal system, GFC is quite unique with the fact that a number of deliberate legal provisions in U.S played an identifiable role is setting the stage for the crisis. Following is a brief discussion on the incentives created by legal provisions in the onset of the GFC.

Law and legal regulation create incentives and disincentives for market participants to behave in particular ways. For example, it was foreshadowed in 2002, in the aftermath of the Enron and WorldCom collapses, that the then-new corporate law reforms United States would be insufficient to control financial conglomerates' perverse incentives for risk-taking, particularly given problems of moral hazard, conflicts of interest, and the incentive of management of distressed institutions to postpone asset write-downs in the hope that their company's financial position might improve before the next disclosure to the investing public [22].

Moreover, market participants respond strategically to these incentives and disincentives, generally optimising utility within the constraints *inter alia* of bounded rationality and market imperfections (e.g. time leads and lags, asymmetric information, or transactions costs). If the law puts in place economic incentives for financial institutions and companies to take on high levels of risk (e.g. through complex financial innovations such as loan securitizations in a rising asset market) and to circumvent relevant legislation and regulation that is in place (e.g. by siphoning funds through offshore entities, or by entering credit default swaps)[6], it is hardly surprising if institutions and companies act on those economic incentives. Moreover, if the incentives created by legislation turn out to be perverse with unintended consequences, then at least some of the responsibility must lie with the legislature, rather than the institutions or companies [23–25].

Changes in the law can empower and disempower vested interests, with each strategic response to the incentives created having costs and benefits for the affected parties. This empowerment and disempowerment, with its attendant costs and benefits, creates winners and losers. Welfare economics investigates not only how to optimise resource allocation for given distributions of income across markets, but the effects of different resource distributions on these winners and losers, and on society generally. One of the ways in which market participants seek to ensure that they become 'winners' out of legislative change, rather than 'losers', is to (legally) circumvent any proscriptions or restrictions on their behaviour [26].

3.2 Uncertainty, information asymmetry, complexity and 'sophisticated' investors

Innovation is, by its nature, often risky. Financial innovation, in the form of asset-backed securities issued under securitization schemes, largely facilitated much of the indirect investment by domestic and overseas institutions in U.S. housing assets [26]. As had conventionally been the case, the purpose of much of this financial innovation was to minimise risk and enhance expected returns by

[6] For example, credit default swaps were outside the ambit of the *Commodity Futures Modernisation Act* 2000 (U.S.) and the *Securities Exchange Act* 1934 (U.S.), with the result that they operated beyond the purview of the U.S. Commodity Futures Trading Commission and, in practice (if not in strict law) the Securities Exchange Commission. Moreover, credit default swaps were specifically excluded from State-based insurance legislation. The justification for credit default swaps lying outside these legislative regimes was that the users of these swaps are institutional (presumably sophisticated) investors, rather than (for example) uninformed consumers [27].

reducing bank funding costs, differentiating fundamentally similar products,[7] and for balance sheet management purposes. In addition however, much of this innovation—in particular, securitization contacts themselves and credit default swaps, which were designed to compensate investors when security issuers defaulted—was designed to transfer credit risk and liquidity risk [4, 5]. Almost by definition, financial innovation implies risk and uncertainty. In general, financial markets can *ex ante* cope with both. For example, risk can be hedged using derivatives; uncertainty can be mitigated using insurance. While neither mechanism can prevent losses occurring *ex post*, they do alleviate the *ex ante* concerns of risk-averse or uncertainty-averse borrowers and investors [28]. Even in an historical point of view, innovative financial instruments are closely associated with asset bubbles. For example the tulip bubble itself is a creative innovation of the day. Yet, not necessarily innovation should be a part of a crisis. The Great Depression associate no financial innovation, but common company stocks.

The transfer of risk and uncertainty downstream is *cet. par.* effective if markets are complete. For example, even if no sub-assignees can be found for a particular securitization asset, financial institutions can readily—at a price—re-bundle the asset into a synthetic collateralized debt obligation (CDO) for which counterparties can be found. Alternatively, if no sub-insurers can be found for the securitization asset, financial institutions can readily—again, at a price—re-bundle derivatives to replicate insurance (analogous to so-called 'portfolio insurance' in funds management) [29, 30].

Problems arise if markets are incomplete[8]—for example, if an institution wishing to sell a particular securitised asset is unable to find a buyer for it, either directly or indirectly. Thus if, in the examples noted earlier, no sub-assignees can be found even for the synthetic CDO, or no investors can be found to participate in the proposed 'insurance replication' then—as with any financial assets that are available for sale but for which no buyer can be found—three consequences follow. First, the risk will not be able to be transferred, since no contract counterparty can be found. This affects who, in the event of significant default or insolvency, is likely to be default losses in respect of the securitised asset. Second, the lack of buyer demand would generally imply price falls for the securitised asset (ultimately to zero).

This highlights the importance of the role of 'market makers' in financial markets. Market makers are so-called because they have sufficient clientele on the buy and sell sides of a trade that they are willing to accept the risk of holding a stock of securities to help facilitate trading (buying and selling) in those securities. All of the high profile investment banks, noted earlier, that experienced distress in the subprime crisis were market makers. If even market makers cannot find buyers for securitised assets and there no buyer demand in the market generally, then the resultant price falls (ultimately to zero) for the securitised asset represents very substantial price risk for upstream investors. As with all products, innovation implies risk.

---

[7] In terms of market structure, banking and investment is characterised by an oligopoly of large firms (eg. market-makers) with a competitive fringe of small firms. The type of product differentiation that occurred with securitisation is consistent with oligopoly theory.

[8] Strictly an economic theory, an incomplete market means a market in which, under certain conditions, the number of state-contingent claims (securities) is less than the number of states of nature. While a wide array of contingent claims is regularly traded against many states of nature (in the form of futures, options, collars, swaps and various types of insurance), the set of outcomes in nature plainly exceeds the set of claims available in the markets, implying that financial markets remain incomplete in spite of impressive innovation in recent times [31].

3.2.1 Uncertainty

Uncertainty is associated with any financial bubble. Financial crises since the 1660s were driven by uncertainty associated with future prices of a particular asset. The GFC was claimed to be a unique event—as the Turner Review in the UK described it, 'the worst financial crisis for a century'—which suggests *uncertainty* as distinct from risk *simpliciter*. Risk in financial markets is distinguishable from uncertainty on the basis that, while risk can be measured objectively, uncertainty cannot [32, 33]. Thus, by definition, risk is measurable, and can be expressed *ex ante* as a probability or a statistical coefficient. This makes it amenable to financial engineering techniques which utilise average returns, statistical variances and co-variances which can be used to help manage risk [34, 35].

In contrast, by definition uncertainty cannot be measured quantitatively, meaning that advances in financial engineering over recent decades are of limited help for companies and boards faced with considerable uncertainty. And as Professor Knight pointed out as early as 1921, the problem with commercial life—and in this context, with evaluating corporate insolvency in particular, is not business risk *per se*, but the fact that any *ex ante* judgments about uncertainty are themselves fraught with uncertainty [33].

Uncertainty is broadly characterised in economic theory as either exogenous or endogenous uncertainty. *Exogenous* uncertainty relates to factors that are exogenous to an institution or company and beyond directors' and management's control, such as the economy falling into recession, the effects of the GFC, or the impact of unanticipated legislative change.[9] This is, at its heart, a rationale for the 'business judgement' rule in corporate law.[10] No economic system can reduce or eliminate exogenous uncertainty. Its adverse impacts on companies can, however, be mitigated by appropriate insurance[11], provided there is insurance to cover the particular uncertainty (a requirement that is by no means always met in incomplete, 'real world' markets). If there is not, the directors and company management are generally forced to recognise the source of the exogenous uncertainty—assuming they are aware of it—as a constraint on its decision-making, and simply do the best they can in the circumstances, 'in the interests of the company as a whole'.

In contrast, *endogenous* uncertainty results from stakeholders' decisions. Examples might include uncertainty about whether and how much bank debt will be rolled over in the face of successive monthly defaults that have breached interest cover and debt covenants; or uncertainty about whether secured creditors will appoint a receiver in these circumstances. Endogenous uncertainty can be reduced to some degree by company management who are prepared to incur the search costs

---

[9] The law itself may also generate uncertainty. For example, the uncertainty resulting from the conflicting incentives in the Australian *Corporations Act* to, on the one hand, continuously disclose reasonable suspicions of insolvency while, on the other hand, simultaneously continuing to try to trade out of difficulty, is itself a prime example.

[10] See for example, Section 180 of the *Corporations Act* (Cth) in Australia; and in a U.S. context, *Aronson v. Lewis*, 473 A.2d 805, 812 (1984); and *Puma v. Marriott*, Del. Ch., 283 A.2d 693, 695 (1971). In concept (though not in law), the business judgement rule could possibly have been used to defend the securitizer in the recent Australian Federal court case of *Wingecarribee Shire Council v Lehman Brothers Australia (in Liq.)* [2012] FCA1028. The Applicant's case was based, however, on allegations of misleading or deceptive conduct, for which the business judgement rule has no application as a defence. This is presumably why the Applicant's lawyers brought the case in those terms, rather than on the basis of a breach of duty of care having caused Council losses.

[11] For example, mortgage insurance in a securitization.

necessary to make more informed decisions, or otherwise decide—since it is within their control—to do something about it. In the face of investor and market ignorance, introducing a high level of complexity into securitized financial products and transactions can amplify the effects of (largely endogenous) uncertainty.[12]

It is important to distinguish between exogenous and endogenous uncertainty if there is any possibility of apportioning any legal culpability (liability) to the various stakeholders in a securitization. There is plainly more scope for using the exogenous uncertainty resulting from the GFC (for example) as the basis of an argument to defend financial institutions' and companies' behaviour in unique, highly uncertain times; and less scope for doing so on the basis of any endogenous uncertainty created as a result of their own decisions. In that regard, financial institutions and companies could be argued to be 'the authors of their own misfortune'.[13]

3.2.2 Information asymmetry

Information asymmetry relates to the fact that different people have different knowledge about the same thing. For example, the borrower buying mortgage insurance typically knows more about her ability to repay her housing loan than the insurance company. She also knows more about the risks of lending to her than the lender. Financial market participants have incentives to create information asymmetries, in order to increase their bargaining power when negotiating on contracts [36]. Information asymmetries can also lead to weak (or ultimately non-existent) markets—even in financial market products [37].

For example, when negotiating for the transfer of risks in securitization schemes with downstream parties, the transferor typically knows more about those risks than the transferee. In any chain of risky asset sales one after another, upstream bidders will expect this, so that part of the benefit of winning 'earlier' contracts is the information rent that becomes valuable when later on-selling. Yet if those risks have been transferred downstream a sufficient number of times, potential transferees may become wary of purchasing (taking on the risk), knowing that they might be successful only if they bid too high a price.[14] Realising that they are more likely to outbid other, more informed bidders only if they bid too much for the contract, uninformed bidders may deliberately under-bid, or not bid at all. If they do not bid enough, the seller will refrain from selling, choosing instead to bear the risk itself.

In this way, the ability to transfer risk downstream may diminish (or even cease), the further downstream the risk has been transferred already. The downstream party who is left bearing the risk may have 'won' the contract, but information asymmetries may well have led to a 'winners' curse', in which the bidders for securitized products were successful simply because they had bid too much [38]. This may arguably be what happened in the months preceding the GFC, when banks refused to roll over debt facilities for AIG and other large U.S. corporates.

---

[12] Much of the Federal Government's *Report of the Parliamentary Inquiry into Financial Products and Services in Australia* (November 2009) was fundamentally concerned with these types of problems: see Parliamentary Joint Committee on Corporations and Financial Services (Nov 2009), *Inquiry into Financial Products and Services in Australia,* Australian Government, Canberra.

[13] Cf. The judgement of the Full Bench of the Australian High Court case of *Wynbergen v Hoyts Corporation* (1997) 149 ALR 25, per Hayne J. at p. 30. See also (1997) 72 ALJR 65; or [1997] HCA 52.

[14] That is, the price may be 'too high' either in the sense that it over-compensates for the level of risk, or (perhaps more likely) in the sense that the bidder still gains, but not by as much as originally anticipated.

3.2.3 Complexity

The GFC is quite unique with the fact that financial innovation of the day (Asset backed securities, Credit default swaps, etc.) are overly complex compared to financial assets associated with previous asset bubbles. In some cases, because of the complexity of the new products, senior management in financial institutions and companies understood little of the investment risks.[15] As Prof. Schwarcz has pointed out, this complexity in financial products did not arise for its own sake, nor did it (necessarily) arise from an intention to obfuscate. It arose in response to investor demands for mechanisms that facilitate the transfer and trading of risk, and for higher risk-adjusted returns [39, 40]. Even if all information about complex securitization structures were fully disclosed to investors, the level of complexity would *cet. par.* have increased the volume of information necessary to understand the investment with certainty. If potential investors (or their agents) with limited time perceived the costs of reading and understanding that complexity to outweigh the incremental benefit, they would have had incentive to resort to simplifying heuristics, such as credit ratings, as substitutes for fully understanding the risks [39];[16] or simply, at a price, outsource (transfer) the risk by engaging an insurer or credit default swap counterparty. Prof. Stiglitz has articulated this argument further, highlighting how the complexity of financial products created by U.S. banks and institutions increased both risk and information asymmetries [41, 42].

Moreover, complexity can have distributional effects. Because of information asymmetry and agency costs[17] which are spread across an interconnected network of contracts both inside and outside the firm, financial intermediaries can extract rents for, and transfer wealth to, themselves by increasing the complexity of new securities and products they issue. As will be seen, there were plainly incentives for rent extraction and wealth transfers in many securitization schemes.

3.3 Suboptimal contracting

In economic terms, a contract is incomplete when it does not specify all parties' rights and responsibilities in every possible situation. More technically, the contract is insufficiently state-contingent, meaning that its terms, whether express (written or oral) or implied, do not cover all of the parties' rights and responsibilities for all of the contingencies that affect the parties [43].

Frequently, though not always,[18] this is due to transactions costs. For example, the *ex-ante* costs of specifying a particular (e.g. remote) contingency in the contract —or equivalently, every possible contingency in the contract—may exceed the *ex-ante* gains from doing so. It may also be because the parties cannot foresee all of the

---

[15] Cf. the Australian Federal Court case of *Wingecarribee Shire Council v Lehman Brothers Australia (in Liq.)* [2012] FCA 1028, in which the Court pointed out that, rather than the documentation surrounding collateralised debt obligations (CDOs) being too complex, the securitizer's liability was grounded in evidence that they failed to provide an adequate explanation of the potential investment risks (eg. from the GFC) to their client Councils. The decision is currently on appeal.

[16] Credit rating agencies' methods of rating structured products such as securitisations are imprecise, subject to errors in data, errors in assumptions and errors in modelling. Further, credit rating agencies do not perform due diligence on the loans underlying securitizations [40].

[17] See below.

[18] For example, a contract may be incomplete because one party has private information about factors that affect the payoff between the parties, and chooses not to share this information with the other contracting parties [44].

contingencies that arise during the course of the contract which affect their welfare [45].[19]

Possibly, the parties to the various contracts comprising securitizations prior to the GFC could not foresee the possibility that underlying asset prices might not continue to rise, but must—at least at some stage—level off or fall. It is probably more likely, however, that the agents for these contracting parties simply perceived the *ex-ante* costs of specifying the various payoffs in the event of underlying asset price falls to exceed the *ex-ante* benefits—particularly if, as a result of their own separate contracting or other legal arrangements,[20] their own assets were protected from litigation risk by downstream parties who would ultimately lose money when the contingency eventuated.

If the contract is insufficiently state-contingent because of asymmetric information (either between the contracting parties *inter se*, or between the contracting parties and external decision-makers such as regulators), moral hazard or adverse selection may be possible.[21] Moral hazard can occur when contractual incompleteness creates incentives for agents to act in their own self-interest at the expense of others, so that they do not bear the full consequences of their actions. In the securitization context, for example, where the quality of the underlying investment may be difficult to ascertain because it is packaged jointly with other investments, it could be optimal for a securitizer, who knows the quality of the underlying investments in the asset pool, to seek to guarantee performance to institutional investors by contracting with a mortgage insurer.[22] Once mortgage insurance is in place, however, the insurance creates a moral hazard problem for the securitizer (or its fund manager), who may no longer manage its asset portfolio with sufficient care and diligence [6, 7].

Another example of moral hazard arises where securitizers and other contracting parties either transfer the risks downstream (e.g. by assigning their rights to another party in exchange for consideration), or enter into credit default swaps as a form of 'insurance' against potential defaults. In either case, a moral hazard problem may be created insofar as the transfer of risk induces the transferors in the securitization chain to *cet. par.* undertake riskier investments or continue to undertake highly risky activities. A similar incentive arises if downstream parties purchase on a 'non-recourse' or 'limited recourse' basis back to upstream parties.

A similar argument applies to the various contracting parties to the extent that they have limited liability. In the event of insolvency, the limited liability of the securitizer and the other contracting parties in the securitization chain *cet. par.* effectively insures these parties against losses that accrue from highly variable market conditions (limiting downside risk), without limiting potential gains. This creates a moral hazard problem insofar as it induces securitizers and others in the securitization chain to *cet. par.* undertake riskier investments.

---

[19] A third possible explanation for contractual incompleteness, though one arguably less relevant in the current context, is that the contracting parties are boundedly rational.

[20] For example, the use of family discretionary trusts; or having key assets in their spouses' or other entities' names.

[21] For the sake of completeness, if the contract related only to trade but not investment, and the parties expected that uncertainty could only be resolved in an efficient way *ex post*, then they could specify an option to renegotiate the contract as a means of achieving efficient outcomes *ex post* [46] In the current context, securitisation contracts involve investment as well as trade, so agreeing to renegotiate (e.g. in the event of an underlying asset price collapse) is generally not a practical alternative.

[22] This also serves to signal 'safety' to investors.

3.3.1 Adverse selection

In any market in which products of different quality are traded, and only sellers know the quality of the products they sell (i.e. there is asymmetric information between buyers and sellers), poor quality products will always be sold with good quality products unless there is some device to buyers to distinguish the good from the bad. In such circumstances, the poor quality products are as likely to be purchased as the good quality products—an outcome of adverse selection.

In an insurance context, those with the greatest risk of loss *cet. par.* have a greater incentive to take out insurance against that loss. Because the applicant for the insurance knows the risks of insuring him better than the insurer, the insurer is unable to adjust the insurance premium accurately to reflect the true level of risk. This gives the insurer an incentive to, among other things, sub-insure to another (downstream) insurer, effectively transferring the risk to the latter at a price.

In a securitisation context, those originators and securitizers with the greatest risk of loss *cet. par.* had the greatest incentive to 'insure' against that loss either through mortgage insurance, transferring the risk by equitably assigning their rights to downstream investors, 'non-recourse' or 'limited recourse' clauses, or credit default swaps. Likewise, mortgage insurers have similar incentives to sub-insure downstream. Provided markets were sufficiently complete and underlying asset prices continued to rise, these strategies were effective. They ceased to be effective when U.S. house prices collapsed and buyers who are willing to bear the risk of losses could no longer be found.

3.4 Lack of accountability and the role of ethics

Put simply, markets and societies in which participants can trust each other because each observes shared ethical norms run more smoothly and efficiently than markets and societies that do not. In economic terms, markets and societies function more efficiently and effectively in the long run if all participants share the same or sufficiently similar ethical norms and values. Problems arise because some individuals and firms operating within markets and societies are able to profit, sometimes hugely, in the short run by engaging in unethical conduct. Since the long run is an accumulation of short runs, individuals and firms who engage in unethical behaviour may survive longer than expected. While it is true that transparency and publicity about the unethical conduct may impair their reputations and result in lower profits, this is by no means guaranteed [47, 48].

Nevertheless, in practice, ethical norms exist as dimensions to financial decision-making. They may sometimes be ignored, but they exist nevertheless. The efficient functioning of markets takes place within the context of the law, which is predicated on an axiology of ethical values such as investor protection, the unfairness of insider trading, and the like. In this sense, law is moral philosophy or ethics in action.[23] Similarly, the regulation of financial markets, firms and institutions is based in the ethical values of the relevant society.

Finance theory cannot escape the relevance of ethics, since many propositions in finance are inherently both positive and normative. For example, the idea that

[23] Having said this, the law is at best a very limited vehicle for ensuring ethical behaviour, for two main reasons. First, lawmaking is generally slow and tends to be reactive in its attempts to solve a social problem. Second, the law cannot be made to cover every 'bad' situation, because it is not possible to predict and outlaw all situations that give rise to 'bad' conduct. Thus, while Birks is correct in asserting that law is moral philosophy or ethics in action, mere compliance with the letter of the law may result in very minimalist ethics in action.

securitizations permit risk transfers, at a price, to downstream parties, has normative (as well as positive) implications if the price paid does not reflect the investment risks. Alternatively, in the context of the GFC, it is natural for people to have some sympathy, based on grounds of morality, for stakeholders whose wealth has been expropriated in—for example—Ponzi schemes or securitization issues that generate wealth transfers between classes of security holders. Likewise, if contagion does spread between firms, markets and even countries, it is natural for people to feel that it is somehow unfair or inequitable for others to be adversely affected through no fault of their own [49].

As suggested by the term 'moral hazard', the government bailouts of financially distressed corporations considered 'too big to fail' have moral implications, not only for the taxpayers who ultimately fund them but the corporations who are their beneficiaries.[24] Similarly, financiers' exploitation of information asymmetries between bankers and small investors through the use of confusing terms such as 'negative equity' and 'bridging equity' in prospectuses has ethical implications for both.

In economics, from which finance theory is in part derived, ethics is normally treated as a 'given', determined with reference to societal norms; and behaviour in firms and markets can be optimised within the bounds imposed by ethical and other constraints, using second best principles if appropriate. Likewise, financial maxima and optima can be discussed only for a given distribution of wealth between relevant parties: investor wealth can be maximised, but only subject to a 'given' constraint determined by the ethical norms of the society in which the firm operates [7, 50].

By way of example, consider the ethical implications of a manager in a financial institution who issues securitized notes that generate wealth transfers between classes of security holders. Assuming ethical behaviour is viewed as good for its own sake, there is a good argument (based on efficiency as much as equity or fairness) that the manager as agent should formulate business and financing policies first with reference to his ethical responsibilities and only secondarily with reference to investor (principal) wealth. Investor wealth could still be maximised, but only subject to a 'given' constraint determined by the ethical norms of the society in which the principal institution or corporation operates. By extension, the distribution of wealth between the institution's various stakeholders (e.g. shareholders, debt holders and management) could still be determined by equilibrium values of bonding costs, monitoring costs and residual loss, but only subject to a similar 'given' ethical constraint, at the limit determined by society (e.g. through regulation and norms of 'acceptable' behaviour).[25]

---

[24] For example, in the context of the AIG bailout by the U.S. Government, Prof. Crotty points to the actions of U.S. Treasury Secretary Henry Paulson, who authorised an investment of $180 billion to protect the value of U.S. corporations who would reportedly have incurred significant losses on derivative and securitization contracts if AIG had been wound up. In the process, Goldman Sachs—of whom Henry Paulson was formerly a Chief Executive—received $12.9 billion. According to Crotty, Paulson must have known that Goldman Sachs would receive billions as a result of his decision, reflecting "moral hazard of the highest order" [51].

[25] As Prof. Little points out, it is such distributional questions that are often the important ones. Yet there is no principle of morality or justice *per se* that determines how much, on average, members of particular groups should receive. A distributional judgement must be made. The question in practice, these days often asked by post-modernists, is "By whom?" In a democracy, there is no general way of resolving this. Prof. Little argues that pluralism in modern democracies is a given, and every case must be decided on its merits. Plainly Arrow's impossibility theorem continues to be of relevance to such distributional issues, notwithstanding the reluctance of some who, like Plato, regard it as perhaps accurate but ultimately not very helpful [50].

3.5 Overconfidence and domestic systemic risk

As Keynes pointed out, economists—let alone practical people in business—tend to assume that the existing state of affairs will continue indefinitely, unless there are specific reasons to expect a change [52].[26]

In the years immediately preceding the sub-prime crisis, there was a widespread belief and overconfidence among households, companies and financial institutions themselves that, for the foreseeable future, interest rates would remain relatively low, liquidity relatively high, and house and other key asset prices would continue to rise [53]. Banks and financial institutions continued to lend, underestimating the timing and extent of any future market collapse. A herd mentality[27] developed, resulting in an irrational exuberance[28] in the markets and a speculative bubble, with the attendant risks of losses in the event of its collapse.

Systemic risk can be defined as:

> *"the risk that an economic shock, such as market or institutional failure, triggers (through a panic or otherwise) either ... the failure of a chain of markets or institutions or ... a chain of significant losses to financial institutions, ... resulting in increases in the cost of capital or decreases in its availability, often evidenced by substantial financial market price volatility" [54].*

Before the sub-prime crisis and the GFC, the United States was the world's largest economy on a GDP basis, and remains so. The U.S. Dollar is the world reserve currency. It is hardly surprising that global investor confidence is largely dependent on the state of U.S. financial markets and the health of the U.S. economy.

When U.S. house prices collapsed in the wake of the sub-prime crisis, and financial institutions globally perceived the riskiness of other financial institutions and companies (so-called counterparty risk) increasing, they lost confidence in each other's credit servicing ability, ceasing not only to continue to purchase residential mortgage-backed securities in the U.S., but also commercial asset-backed and non-asset-backed securities in the U.S. and elsewhere.

The network interconnectedness of bank finance globally can, in the event of a sufficient economic shock, transmit to a broader systemic shock if a sufficient number of banks (or sufficiently important banks) make sufficient losses that they themselves become unable to service their debts, not only to their depositors but to other banks. In the wake of the sub-prime crisis, the loss of confidence in the wholesale markets had the effect of reducing the supply of inter-bank credit, which in turn reduced the availability of credit in retail markets, and contributed to the collapse of the real economy in the United States [55, 56].

3.6 Cross-border securitization as regulatory 'arbitrage'

Investment opportunities may plainly expanded by not limiting securitization arrangements to one domestic jurisdiction, but by engaging in cross-border or

---

[26] Keynes further argued that, by its very nature, entrepreneurship must always remain partly skill and partly chance: if human nature had no inclination to take risks, there might not be much long-term investment.

[27] A herd mentality arises when every market participant, knowing that everybody (including themselves) has incomplete information about the value of a particular behaviour, rationally (*ex-ante*) interprets others' consistent prior choices as evidence of the value of that behaviour, and replicates it [57].

[28] Shiller R.J. (2005), *Irrational Exuberance*, Crown, New York.

international securitization. Equally however, the ability to securitize across international borders creates incentives to not only 'arbitrage' on domestic regulation, but to 'arbitrage' on an international network of legal rules.

Prior to the GFC, most securitization schemes exploited regulatory regime inconsistences existed among jurisdictions via cross border securitization in order to bypass the existing regulations. In order to make assets isolated from its originator, then practice was to transfer all assets to a SPV. As a result assets will be bankruptcy remote from its originator, which is essential for securitization to work. A SPV is a different entity from its originator. If both the originator and the SPV are in the same jurisdiction, they will be treated as two distinct companies and will be taxed separately. The innovative solution cross boarder securitizer came up with is to set up SPV in tax heavens like Cayman island to avoid U.S tax regulations. As a result, SPV and the originator could avoid US tax regulation, by being two different business entities while on the other hand can reap the benefits of being a separate entity (that is isolating assets from its originator). When a SPV is setup in another jurisdiction it could bypass the U.S Internal Revenue code of 1986, since the SPV is not an entity engaged in U.S trade or business [58].

Banks were able to transfer their risky assets off balance sheet by transferring them to a SVP. As a result banks were able to by-pass the need for reserves. Banks were able to grant more loans and sell them in the same way. In this manner risk could be shifted off-balance sheet and off shoe.

The off-balance-sheet or on-balance-sheet position of an asset depends on the fact wheatear the asset 'transfer' constitutes a sale or is a loan. This is an issue to be dealt with Accounting. Financial Accounting Standard No. 140 identifies elements of a true sale.[29] If a SPV to come under FAS 140, it will be considered a qualified SPV and thus need not to include in sponsor's consolidated statements.

3.7 Was pre-GFC securitization law suboptimal?

The U.S Commodity Futures Modernization Act 2000 prohibited Securities and Exchange Commission (SEC) and the Commodity Futures Trading Commission (CFTC) regulating Over-the-counter derivatives. The justification is that CDS and similar (over the counter) instruments are transacted by sophisticated parties who can fend themselves and thus there is no need to safeguard such transactions by the SEC and CFTC. Similarly, CDS were (deliberately) not considered insurance contracts. Thus avoided state insurance regulations. State of New York amended the insurance law to exclude CDOs from coverage. The justification is that CDS are dealing with institutional investors but not consumers [4, 27].

---

[29] 1. The transferred assets have been isolated from the transferor—put presumptively beyond the reach of the transferor and its creditors, even in bankruptcy or other receivership.

2. Each transferee (or, if the transferee is qualifying special-purpose entity (SPE), each holder of its beneficial interests) has the right to pledge or exchange the assets (or beneficial interests) it received, and no condition both constrains the transferee (or holder) from taking advantage of its right to pledge or exchange and provides more than a trivial benefit to the transferor.

3. The transferor does not maintain effective control over the transferred assets through either (1) an agreement that both entitles and obligates the transferor to repurchase or redeem them before their maturity or (2) the ability to unilaterally cause the holder to return specific assets, other than through a clean-up call.

See Summary of Statement No. 140, Accounting for Transfers and Servicing of Financial Assets and Extinguishments of Liabilities-a replacement of FASB Statement No. 125 (Issued 9/00), Financial Accounting Standards Board. Online <http://www.fasb.org/summary/stsum140.shtml&pf=true>

On one hand CDSs were not regulated as insurance enabling non-insurable interest holders gaining protection over default of an entity, ultimately leading to betting. On the other hand no authority was overseeing the process. As a result when sup-prime borrowers defaulted, the loss was passed to the investor and then to the CDS provider. Near bankruptcy of AIG is the classic example of risk transfer from the lender to the insurer via the investor. Finally when AIG was bailout, the loss was actually shifted to the U.S treasury in lieu of tax payer [27].

4. Summary

This chapter has sought to provide a contextual background to those that follow. The effects of excess system liquidity and easy credit conditions, executive compensation arrangements which encouraged excessive risk-taking (e.g. through financial innovations such as loan securitization), banking and investment activity that sought to circumvent extant regulation, and the bursting of the U.S. housing bubble together culminated in the U.S. sub-prime crisis. Further, because many U.S. institutions and corporates had entered into contracts (e.g. securitization contracts, insurance/sub-insurance contracts, and credit default swaps) which spanned jurisdictions, the effects of what would otherwise have been a primarily U.S. sub-prime crisis were felt beyond the United States, in Britain and elsewhere in Europe.

This chapter identified and described the salient or root causes of the GFC. Law and legal regulation create incentives and disincentives for market participants to behave in particular ways. A desire for innovation, fuelled by high levels of system liquidity and executive compensation arrangements that encouraged management to undertake high levels of risk, together with a speculative bubble in the U.S. housing market and incomplete regulation, gave rise to highly complex financial products. In the presence of asymmetric information, this complexity gave rise to uncertainty and incomplete contracting, which featured significant moral hazard and adverse selection. Overconfidence in a rising market and lapses of ethical judgement when faced with incomplete regulation resulted, with the collapse of the U.S. housing bubble, in a loss of confidence in U.S. markets, contributing to systemic risk and so-called cross-jurisdictional 'contagion'. Whether this so-called 'contagion' is true contagion or mere contractual interdependence between institutions in different jurisdictions, is a separate matter.

As far as policy implications are concerned, regulating asset backed securities and associated derivatives would be a *prima facie* solution for the mortgage crisis. Yet, there should be wide financial policies to prevent a similar crisis, since; next time it would be some other asset that may create the asset bubble. Financial intelligence units of each individual nation should extend their scope in order to monitor developments in financial bubbles. Like in China, any innovative financial instrument should be registered with financial intelligence units and their mechanism should be analyses and measured in terms of financial safely of the innovation.

There will be no permanent solution to prevent a future for a financial crisis. All we can (and should) do is to avoid financial bubbles that may lead to a crisis. We never know when it would be the next crisis. Yet, we ought to know at least a few things. We know for a fact that it would be some financial asset that will create an asset bubble. There will be associated factors that may contribute to the creation of the bubble. For example financial innovation, law create incentives, etc. All we got to do is keeping an open eye on associated factors and their movements. Global regulation such as BASEL accords can influence individual financial systems to take necessary regulatory measures to regulate and control associated factors of a financial crisis.

Author details

Shanuka Senarath
Department of Economics, University of Colombo, Colombo, Sri Lanka

*Address all correspondence to: shanuka.senarath@griffithuni.edu.au

References

[1] Allen F, Carletti E. The role of liquidity in financial crises. Available at: SSRN 1268367. [Accessed: 04 September 2008]

[2] Sorkin AR. JP Morgan Pays $2 a Share for Bear Stearns. New York: The New York Times; 2008

[3] Omarova ST. Wall street as community of fate: Toward financial industry self-regulation. University of Pennsylvania Law Review. 2010;**159**:411

[4] Senarath S, Copp R. Credit default swaps and the global financial crisis: Reframing credit default swaps as quasi-insurance. Global Economy and Finance Journal. 2015;**8**(1):135-149

[5] Senarath S. The Dodd-Frank Act doesn't solve the principal-agent problem in asset securitisation. LSE Business Review; 2017

[6] Senarath S. Not so 'bankruptcy-remote': An insight into Sri Lankan securitization practices in a Post_GFC context. In: Multidisciplinary Academic Conference on Management, Marketing and Economics. Prague: MAC Prague consulting Ltd; 2016. pp. 53-60

[7] Senarath S. Securitisation and the global financial crisis: Can risk retention prevent another crisis? International Journal of Business and Globalisation. 2017;**18**(2):153-166

[8] Gori M, Witten I. The bubble of web visibility. Communications of the ACM. 2005;**48**(3):115-117

[9] Wicke J. Appreciation, depreciation: Modernism's speculative bubble. Modernism/Modernity. 2001;**8**(3): 389-403

[10] Temin P, Voth HJ. Riding the south sea bubble. American Economic Review. 2004;**94**(5):1654-1668

[11] White EN. Lessons from the Great American Real Estate Boom and Bust of the 1920s. Chicago: National Bureau of Economic Research; 2009

[12] Malpezzi S, Wachter S. The role of speculation in real estate cycles. Journal of Real Estate Literature. 2005;**13**(2): 141-164

[13] Rappoport P, White EN. Was there a bubble in the 1929 stock market? The Journal of Economic History. 1993; **53**(3):549-574

[14] White EN. Stock market bubbles? A reply. The Journal of Economic History. 1995;**55**(3):655-665

[15] Garber PM. Famous first bubbles. Journal of Economic Perspectives. 1990; **4**(2):35-54

[16] McCarty N, Poole KT, Rosenthal H. Political Bubbles: Financial Crises and the Failure of American Democracy. New Jersey: Princeton University Press; 2013

[17] Allen F, Carletti E. The role of liquidity in financial crises. 2008. Available at: SSRN 1268367.

[18] Keynes JM. The general theory of employment. The Quarterly Journal of Economics. 1936;**51**:209-223

[19] Giles MJ. A participatory teaching strategy: Developing a timeline of the global financial crisis

[20] Mendoza EG. Sudden stops, financial crises, and leverage. American Economic Review. 2010;**100**(5):1941-1966

[21] Cohen HR. Preventing the fire next time: Too big to fail. Texas Law Review. 2011;**90**:1717

[22] Wilmarth AE. How should we respond to the growing risks of financial conglomerates? 2002

[23] Koumakhov R. Conventions in Herbert Simon's theory of bounded rationality. Journal of Economic Psychology. 2009;**30**(3):293-306

[24] Tversky A, Kahneman D. Judgment under uncertainty: Heuristics and biases. Science. 1974;**185**(4157): 1124-1131

[25] Kaldor N. Welfare propositions of economics and interpersonal comparisons of utility. The Economic Journal. 1939;**49**:549-552

[26] Simkovic M. Competition and crisis in mortgage securitization. Indiana Law Journal. 2013;**88**:213

[27] Sjostrom WK Jr. The AIG bailout. Washington and Lee Law Review. 2009; **66**:943

[28] Alchian AA. Uncertainty, evolution, and economic theory. Journal of Political Economy. 1950;**58**(3):211-221

[29] Black F, Rouhani R. In: Fabozzi FJ, editor. Constant Proportion Portfolio Insurance and the Synthetic Put Option: A Comparison. Cambridge, Mass: Institutional Investor focus on Investment Management, Ballinger; 1989. pp. 695-708

[30] Black F, Jones R. Simplifying portfolio insurance. Journal of Portfolio Management. 1987;**14**(1):48

[31] Arrow KJ. The role of securities in the optimal allocation of risk-bearing. In: Readings in Welfare Economics. Palgrave Macmillan, London; 1973. pp. 258-263

[32] Turner A. The Turner review: a regulatory response to the global banking crisis. Financial Services Authority. Available from: www.fsa.gov.uk/pages/Library/Corporate/turner/index.shtml 2009

[33] Knight FH. Risk, uncertainty and profit. In: Courier Corporation. Cambridge: Dover Publications, Inc; 2012

[34] Sharpe W, Alexander GJ, Bailey JW. Investments

[35] Copeland TE, Weston JF, Shastri K. Financial Theory and Corporate Policy. Reading, MA: Addison-Wesley; 1988

[36] Edlin AS, Stiglitz JE. Discouraging rivals: Managerial rent-seeking and economic inefficiencies. The American Economic Review. 1995;**85**(5):1301-1312

[37] Stiglitz JE, Weiss A. Credit rationing in markets with imperfect information. The American Economic Review. 1981; **71**(3):393-410

[38] Wilson R. Competitive Bidding with Disparate Information. Graduate School of Business, Stanford University; 1966

[39] Schwarcz SL. Regulating complexity in financial markets. Washington University Law Review. 2009;**87**:211

[40] Partnoy F. The paradox of credit ratings. In: Ratings, Rating Agencies and the Global Financial System. Boston, MA: Springer; 2002. pp. 65-84

[41] Roe M. The derivatives players' payment priorities as financial crisis accelerator'. Stanford Law Review. 2011;**63**:539

[42] Stiglitz JE. Freefall: America, Free Markets, and the Sinking of the World Economy. New York: WW Norton & Company; 2010

[43] Tirole J. Incomplete contracts: Where do we stand? Econometrica. 1999;**67**(4):741-781

[44] Allen F, Gale D. Measurement distortion and missing contingencies in optimal contracts. Economic Theory. 1992;**2**(1):1-26

[45] Williamson OE. The economic institutions of capitalism. Firms,

markets, relational contracting. In: Das Summa Summarum des Management. Wiesbaden: Gabler; 2007. pp. 61-75

[46] Schwartz A, Watson J. The law and economics of costly contracting. Journal of Law, Economics, and Organization. 2004;**20**(1):2-31

[47] O'Brien J. Redesigning Financial Regulation: The Politics of Enforcement. West Sussex: John Wiley & Sons; 2006

[48] Kapur BK. Harmonization between communitarian ethics and market economics. Journal of Markets & Morality. 1999;**2**(1):35-52

[49] Drew JM, Drew ME. The identification of Ponzi schemes: Can a picture tell a thousand frauds? Griffith Law Review. 2010;**19**(1):51-70

[50] Little IM. A Critique of Welfare Economics. Oxford: OUP; 2002

[51] Crotty J. Structural causes of the global financial crisis: A critical assessment of the 'new financial architecture'. Cambridge Journal of Economics. 2009;**33**(4):563-580

[52] Keynes JM. The General Theory of Employment, Interest, and Money. Cham: Palgrave Macmillan; 2018

[53] Vasile D, Sebastian TC. Radu T. a behavioral approach to the global financial crisis. Economic. Science. 2011; **20**(2):340-346

[54] Schwarcz SL. Systemic risk. The Georgetown Law Journal. 2008;**97**:193

[55] Alexander K, Dhumale R, Eatwell J. Global Governance of Financial Systems: The International Regulation of Systemic Risk. Oxford: Oxford University Press; 2005

[56] Anabtawi I, Schwarcz SL. Regulating systemic risk: Towards an analytical framework. Notre Dame Law Review. 2011;**86**:1349

[57] Bikhchandani S, Hirshleifer D, Welch I. A theory of fads, fashion, custom, and cultural change as informational cascades. Journal of Political Economy. 1992;**100**(5): 992-1026

[58] Kothari V. Securitization: The Financial Instrument of the Future. Singapore: John Wiley & Sons (Asia) pte Ltd; 2006

Section 5

Financial Crisis: A Case on Turkey

Chapter 5

External Factors on Turkish Short-Term Interest Rates and Daily Exchange Rates: Tranquil Periods versus Politically Stressed Times

Dogus Emin

Abstract

This chapter studies the impacts of short-term interest rates of United States and emerging markets risk premia as external factors on Turkish short-term interest rates and daily exchange rates during the period of January 2011–December 2018. Following Edwards and Borensztein et al., we construct a vector autoregressive (VAR) model with the domestic short-term interest rates, exchange rate against the US Dollar, the US interest rates and iShares MSCI emerging markets ETF. Hereby, we intend to shed some light on the reaction of Turkish interest rates and exchange rates to the short-term US interest rates and emerging markets instability. As other emerging countries, Turkey is rather economically and politically unstable country. Even a little political development may cause a serious volatility in the market. For that reason, in this study we specifically examine the periods that are known as politically stressed times and tranquil periods separately to see how external factors' behaviors change during shock periods.

Keywords: interest rate contagion, exchange rate, VAR model, financial crisis, emerging markets

1. Introduction

The risk exposures from the US during the 2007–2009 financial crisis spread rapidly to the global financial markets and gradually increased its severity while the great number of banks bankrupted due to increase in interest rates. The major role for the bankruptcies of the banks in European countries was the domino effect of the spread of interest rate risk in the interbank market and liquidity risk (e.g., [1, 2]). Since the liquidity risks correspond to counterparty risk, the idiosyncratic credit problems arising from the US subprime mortgage market spread rapidly to other countries through the channels of changes in interest rate (e.g., [2–5]). Brunnermeier and Pedersen [3] empirically show that increase in interest rates affect the financial institutions that have liquidity problems as those institutions are more open to risk contagion arising from the interest rate rise. "For this reason, banks, which carry interbank credit risk threats, are exposed to liquidity risks and such a systemic risk contagion causes subsequent bankruptcies (see e.g., [6–11])" ([12], p. 243).

Even though the existing literature mainly addresses the issues such as risk contagion across stock markets or foreign exchange markets due to counterparty relationships, macroeconomic risk or financial linkages; how interest rate risk propagates around global financial markets is not fully investigated (e.g., [10, 13–15]). As interest rates can be used domestically to absorb the external shocks and to balance the currency, the propagation of the interest rate risks between financial markets gains much more importance for economically semi- and fully open countries.

How foreign interest rates and the exchange rates affect the domestic interest rates can be shown with the following equation:

$$i_t = i_t^* + E_t e_{t+1} - e_t + \pi_t \tag{1}$$

where i_t is the domestic interest rate with maturity $t + 1$; i_t^* is the foreign interest rates with the same maturity; e_t is the natural logarithm of the spot exchange rate at time t; and π_t is the country risk premium. According to this, every shock to i^* or π can be absorbed by changes in domestic interest rates and changes in the expected rate of depreciation. Therefore, it is possible to say that under floating exchange rate regime, policy makers have freedom to increase or decrease the domestic interest rates to adjust the exchange rate. For example, "a positive shock to i^* or π may cause an immediate devaluation of the exchange rate which overshoots its long-run equilibrium and tends to appreciate (or reduce its rate of depreciation)" ([16], p. 7). In other words, under floating exchange rate regime, flexible exchange rate can absorb external shocks.

According to Edwards [17], the interest rate spread, which can be defined as the difference between lending and riskless rates, is a key transmission channel for interest rate risk propagation (e.g., [5, 18–20]). Borensztein et al. [21] examine the impact of international interest rate shocks and emerging market risk premia on domestic interest rates and exchange rates for both emerging and developed countries. The authors find different results for Latin American and Asian economies and for different exchange rate regimes. According to that in Mexico and Argentina, emerging market risk premia significantly affects the interest rates. On the other hand, the Asian countries show different reactions according to their exchange rate regimes; Singapore which has a floating exchange rate regime seems unaffected by the external shocks while Hong Kong responses significantly to the emerging market risk premia.

There are more recent papers that investigate the impacts of external shocks for various countries. In Ref. [22], Demirel investigates the impulse responses of the Turkish economy to the US interest rate shocks. The study reveals that Turkey is less sensitive to the interest rate shocks while she has lower levels of external debt. Therefore, the author concludes that the foreign interest rate shocks depend on the level of external debt for small-open economies. Allegret et al. [23] examine the relative importance of external shocks in domestic fluctuations for East Asian countries. Using a structural VAR model, the authors show that real oil price and the US GDP shocks have significant impacts on domestic activity. They also reveal that since the mid-1990s, external shocks have rising impacts on domestic variables in those countries. Using a trend-cycle VAR model, Andrle et al. [24] investigate how external factors affect the Poland's domestic variables. According to that, the authors reach the conclusion that about 50% of Poland's output and interest rate variance and about 25% of the variance of inflation can be explained with shocks from Euro zone. Pelipas et al. [25] test the significance of Russia's GDP and oil prices as the external factors on Belarus' economy. Using generalized impulse response functions, the authors show that oil prices have strong and negative impact on the economy while Russia's GDP does not have that strong impact.

This chapter is motivated to some extent by the earlier work of Edwards [26] and Borensztein et al. [21]. Therefore, following those studies, in this study, I aim to construct a vector auto regression (VAR) model to examine the effect of external shocks on Turkish short-term interest rates and the exchange rate. Differently from Edwards [26] and Borensztein et al. [21] and the more recent papers, I investigate how the impact of external shocks change according to tranquil and politically stressed periods as Turkey is a rather politically instable country and this situation causes authorities to interfere with the floating exchange rate regime every now and then.

The chapter is structured as follows. Section 2 presents data we use to analyze the impacts of external shocks on the Turkish short-term interest rates and the exchange rate; and the VAR model under Section 2.2. Section 3 reports the estimation results according to full period, each politically stressed periods and the politically tranquil periods. Finally, the wrap up of the results and conclusions are offered in Section 4.

2. Data and methodology

2.1 Data

The time period, in this study, is determined as January 2011–December 2018. Turkey has been governed by one political party since 2002. Therefore, the period from 2002 to today can be counted as a rather politically stable period for Turkey. However, in our study we do not want to include the first 5 years of the AKP (The Justice and Development Party) governments as this period can be counted as the rebalancing and redevelopment period after the heavy financial crisis of 2001. Furthermore, as during the years between 2007 and 2010, global financial crisis may have a dominant role on the markets instead of local developments, we do not include this period into our study too. Therefore, the period that we decide to examine, 2011–2018, solely shows us the impact of external factors change on the short-term interest rates and the daily exchange rates according to politically stressed times or tranquil periods.

In this study, 3-months interbank rates are used as the short-term interest rates. To be able to assess how group of emerging countries affect Turkish domestic interest rates and the exchange rates, daily iShares MSCI emerging markets ETF is used as the proxy of the emerging market risk premia (difference between return of a risky asset and the risk-free rate). Finally for the exchange rate, daily spot exchange rate against the US Dollar is used. Therefore, our data set includes daily 3-months interbank interest rates for Turkey and the US, daily iShares MSCI emerging markets ETF and daily spot exchange rate against the US Dollar for Turkish Lira.

Data set covers the period January 1, 2011–December 31, 2018 for a total of 2087 daily observations and is downloaded from Bloomberg Terminal. **Figure 1** represents the graphs of each group of data for the examined period.

In **Figure 1**, the first graph presents how USD/TRY exchange rate changes between 2011 and 2019. Second and third graphs present the pattern of short-term interest rates for USA and Turkey between 2011 and 2019. The final graph shows how emerging market risk premium changes during the 2011–2019 period.

To be able to determine the politically stressed times that have significant impacts on the financial markets of Turkey, we identify the financial stress periods. For this purpose, we first identify the anomalies on the daily price changes on Borsa

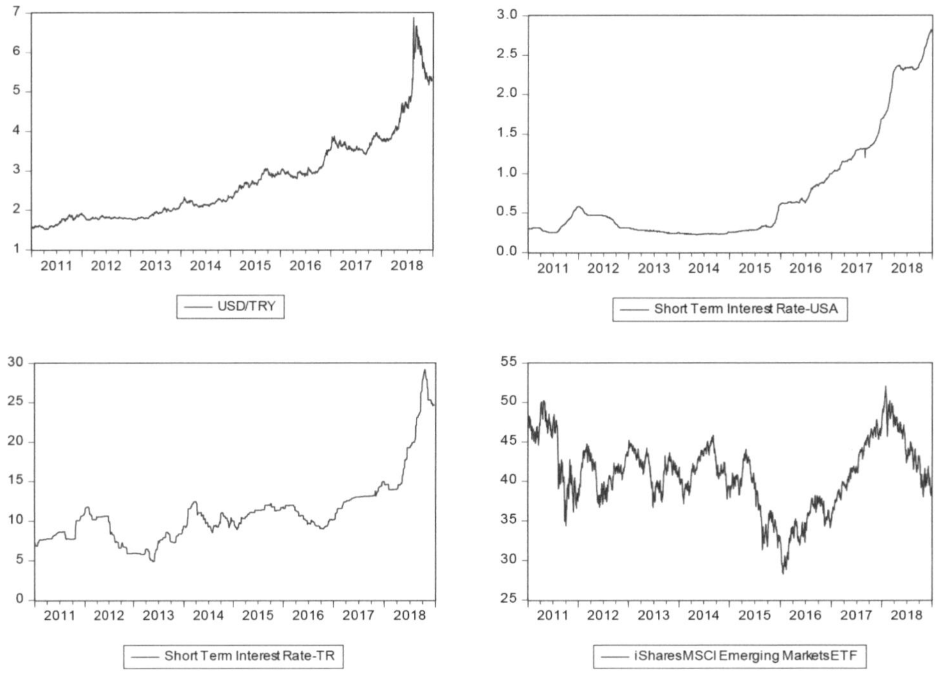

Figure 1.
Exchange rates in Turkey, interest rates in Turkey and the US and emerging markets risk premia (2011–2019).

Istanbul. We define the anomalies as 5% or above drop on the main index of Borsa Istanbul in total in at least 5 days period.

Financial markets experience either a crash or a bear market. The widely used criteria for a crash is 10% drop from the peak prices in 1 or 2 days and a drop of at least 20% off peak prices in a wider time period for the bear market. While identifying the price anomalies in Turkish market, we consider both of those criteria. To be able to decide on the exact drop rate, we examine the sharp drops in Borsa Istanbul for 20 years period. During that period, the average correction rate for the market is calculated as 3.7%. Therefore to able to identify a price movement as an anomaly, we need to determine a rate above this rate. However, as we do not want to keep that rate as high as a rate that is needed to classify the drop as a stock crash, we identify 5% and above rates as price anomalies. Finally, as we determine that Borsa Istanbul shows the strongest reactions to negative events or news in the first 5 days on average, we decide on the 5 days criterion.

After the examination of the daily price changes of Borsa Istanbul from 2011 till 2019, we identify eight different periods that BIST100 lose at least 5% in total in at least 5 days.

Following the identification of the financial stress periods, we identify the domestic political developments that occur on the same periods. These are;

- 10 days period which starts with the early retirement request of commanders of Turkish Army on 29th July 2011,
- 3 weeks period which starts with Gezi Park incidents on 28th May 2013,
- 1 month period which starts with the operation of FETO terror organization to government authorities on 17th December 2013,
- 10 days period which starts on 31st July 2014 prior to presidential election,

- the period which starts with the 7th June 2015 general elections and continues until the announcement of new elections on 25th August 2015,
- 2 weeks period which starts with the shootdown of Russian plane on Turkish border on 24th November 2015,
- 2 weeks period which starts with the military coup attempt on 15th July 2016,
- 3 months period which starts with the announcement of new cabinet on 2nd July 2018 and strengthens with Pastor Branson's house arrest and ends with Brunson's return to USA.

To be able to show the relation between short-term interest rates of USA, short-term interest rates of Turkey and USD/TRY exchange rate, we prepare **Figure 2**. Although the figure does not allow us to statistically prove the correlation between the US interest rates, Turkish interest rates and USD/TRY exchange rate; it is still possible to see that especially in the latter period (after 2017) short-term interest rates of USA, short-term interest rates of Turkey and USD/TRY share significant common pattern.

Figure 2 presents the graphs of the short-term interest rates for both US and Turkey and the USD/TRY exchange rate for the 2011–2019 period.

Differently from **Figure 2**, **Figure 3** brings emerging risk premia and short-term interest rates of Turkey and USD/TRY exchange rate together to show whether Turkish risky assets and emerging markets risk premia share common pattern during the examined period.

Figure 3 presents the graphs of iShares MSCI Emerging Markets ETF, Turkish short-term interest rate and USD/TRY exchange rate for the 2011–2019 period.

2.2 Methodology

In this chapter, to be able to examine the effect of US interest rates and emerging market risk premia on the domestic short-term interest rate of Turkey and exchange rate against the US Dollar, we construct a vector auto regression (VAR) model. More specifically, the model includes the Turkish short-term interest rate, the US short-term interest rate, the natural logarithm of the exchange rate against the US dollar and iShares MSCI emerging markets ETF. We expect to see that during the tranquil periods, the Turkish short-term interest rate and the USD/TRY exchange rate are both positively and significantly affected by the US short-term interest rate and the emerging market risk premia. According to that, we expect to see that short-term Turkish interest rate and the USD/TRY exchange rate increase with the increasing short-term US interest rate and the emerging market risk

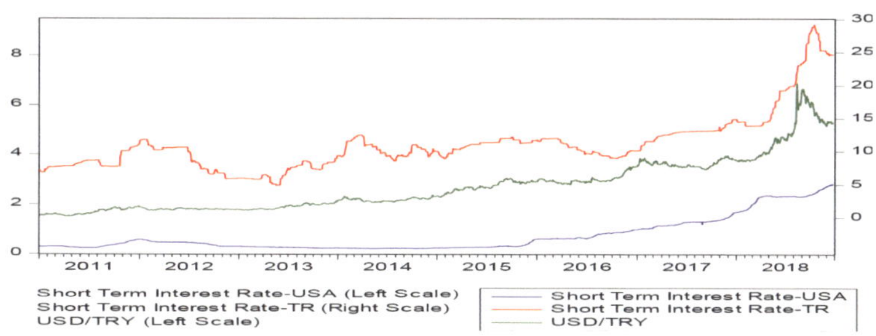

Figure 2.
Short-term interest rate of USA, short-term interest rate of Turkey and USD/TRY exchange rate.

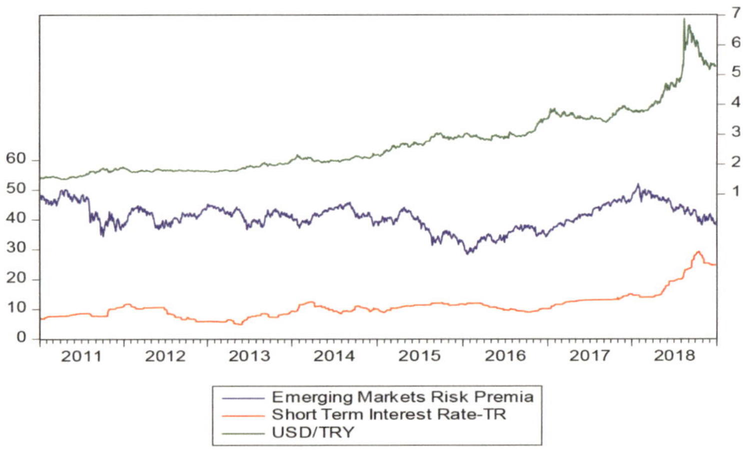

Figure 3.
Emerging markets risk premia, short-term interest rate of Turkey and USD/TRY.

premia. However, during the politically stressed periods it is not possible to estimate the relations between those variables as each political stress may have a different impact according to their dynamics. For instance, while a fully domestic political stress may cause Turkish financial markets to separate from the rest of the world, a political stress that is caused by an international development may cause Turkish markets to more sensitive to the external shocks.

"The vector autoregression (VAR) model is one of the most successful, flexible, and easy to use models for the analysis of multivariate time series" ([27], p. 385). It is a natural extension of the univariate autoregressive model to dynamic multivariate time series.[1]

Let $Y_t = (y_{1t}, y_{2t}, \ldots, y_{nt})'$ denote an $(n \times 1)$ vector of time series variables. The basic *p-lag* vector autoregressive model has the form;

$$Y_t = \mathrm{c} + \Pi_1 Y_{t-1} + \Pi_2 Y_{t-2} + \ldots + + \Pi_p Y_{t-p} + \varepsilon_t,\ t = 1, \ldots, T \qquad (2)$$

where Π_i are $(n \times n)$ coefficient matrices and ε_t is an $(n \times 1)$ unobservable zero mean White noise vector process with time invariant covariance matrix Σ. According to this, for example, a bivariate VAR(2) model equation by equation has the form;

$$y_{1t} = c_1 + \pi_{11}^1 Y_{1t-1} + \pi_{12}^1 Y_{2t-1} + \pi_{11}^1 Y_{1t-2} + \pi_{12}^2 Y_{2t-2} + \varepsilon_{1t} \qquad (3)$$

$$y_{2t} = c_1 + \pi_{21}^1 Y_{1t-1} + \pi_{22}^1 Y_{2t-1} + \pi_{21}^1 Y_{1t-1} + \pi_{22}^2 Y_{2t-1} + \varepsilon_{2t} \qquad (4)$$

where $cov(\varepsilon_{1t}, \varepsilon_{2t}) = \sigma_{12}$. Each equation has the same regressors-lagged values of y_{1t} and y_{2t}. Hence the VAR(p) model is just a seemingly unrelated regression (SUR) model with lagged variables and deterministic terms as common regressors.

In lag operator notation, the VAR(p) is written as;

$$\Pi(L)Y_t = \mathrm{c} + \varepsilon_t \qquad (5)$$

where $\Pi(L) = I_n - \Pi_1 L - \ldots - \Pi_p L^p$. The VAR(p) is stable if the roots of

[1] The theoretical presentation of vector autoregressive models that is used in the Methodology part is taken from the book of Zivot and Wang [26].

$$det\left(I_n - \Pi_1 z - \dots - \Pi_p z^p\right) = 0 \tag{6}$$

lie outside the complex unit circle (have modulus greater than one), or, equivalently, if the eigenvalues of the companion matrix have modules less than one. Assuming that the process has been initialized in the infinite past, then a stable VAR (p) process is stationary and ergodic with time invariant means, variances and autocovariances.

If Y_t is covariance stationary, then the unconditional mean is given by;

$$\mu = \left(I_n - \Pi_1 - \dots - \Pi_p\right)^{-1} c \tag{7}$$

The mean-adjusted form of the VAR(p) is then;

$$Y_t - \mu = \Pi_1(Y_{t-1} - \mu) + \Pi_2(Y_{t-2} - \mu) + \dots + \Pi_p\left(Y_{t-p} - \mu\right) + \varepsilon_t \tag{8}$$

The general form of the VAR(p) model with deterministic terms and exogenous variables is given by;

$$Y_t = \Pi_1 Y_{t-1} + \Pi_2 Y_{t-2} + \dots + \Pi_p Y_{t-p} + \phi D_t + G X_t + \varepsilon_t \tag{9}$$

where D_t represents an $(l \times 1)$ matrix of deterministic components, X_t represents an $(m \times 1)$ matrix of exogenous variables, and ϕ and G are parameter matrices.

To be able to estimate the basic VAR(p) model, each equation in the model can be written as;

$$y_i = Z\pi_i + e_i,\ i = 1, \dots, n \tag{10}$$

where y_i is a $(T \times 1)$ vector of observations on the ith equation, Z is a $(T \times k)$ matrix with tth row given by $Z'_t = \left(1, Y'_{t-1}, \dots, Y'_{t-p}\right), k = np + 1, \pi_i$ is a $(k \times 1)$ vector of parameters and e_i is a $(T \times 1)$ error with covariance matrix $\sigma_i^2 I_T$. Since the VAR(p) is in the form of a SUR model where each equation has the same explanatory variables, each equation may be estimated separately by ordinary least squares without losing efficiency relative to generalized least squares.

3. Results

In this study, to be able to show how the impact of external shocks on domestic interest rates and the exchange rates change according to political stress in Turkey, we construct a VAR model. **Figure 4** plots interest rates and exchange rates in Turkey over the period of 2011–2019. The politically stressed periods are highlighted on this figure to show how domestic interest rates and exchange rates react to political developments. Therefore, eight shaded lines on **Figure 4** identify the following major political crises in Turkey;

- 10 days period which starts with the early retirement request of commanders of Turkish Army on 29th July 2011,
- 3 weeks period which starts with Gezi Park incidents on 28th May 2013,
- 1 month period which starts with the operation of FETO terror organization to the government authorities on 17th December 2013,

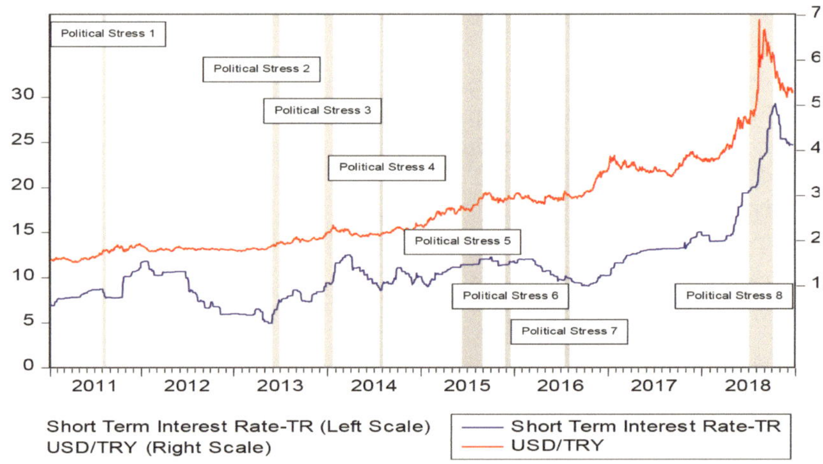

Figure 4.
Short-term interest rates and spot exchange rate in Turkey.

- 10 days period which starts on 31st July 2014 prior to presidential election,
- The period which starts with the 7th June 2015 general elections and continues until the announcement of new elections on 25th August 2015,
- 2 weeks period which starts with the shootdown of Russian plane on Turkish border on 24th November 2015,
- 2 weeks period which starts with the military coup attempt on 15th July 2016,
- 3 months period which starts with the announcement of new cabinet on 2nd July 2018 and strengthens with Pastor Branson's house arrest and ends with Brunson's return to USA.

Figure 4 presents the graphs of Turkish short-term interest rates and the USD/TRY exchange rate for the period of 2011–2019. **Figure 4** also highlights the political stress periods to show how interest rate and exchange rate react to the political stresses.

Figure 4 highlights the political stress periods to show how short-term interest rates and the USD/TRY pair react to the political stresses. As it can be clearly seen from the graph, most of the time political crises coincide with the sharp depreciation of the Turkish Lira against the US Dollar, while interest rates seem to react shortly after the political crises. Political stress #8 which starts with the lawsuit of Pastor Branson seems to have the most remarkable impact on Turkish interest rates which causes a rise from around 17% to above 25%. According to **Figure 4**, Turkish Lira significantly depreciates and short-term interest rates significantly increase in the fourth quarter of 2011, the first quarter of 2017 and the fourth quarter of 2017. However, as we did not identify any political crisis during those periods, we are not in a position to relate these drastic moves with any political stress.

We use VAR analysis to model the behaviour of domestic interest rates and nominal exchange rates. By doing so while our main target is detecting the impact of external shocks on these variables, by identifying the major politically stress periods we also aim to see how political stress makes changes on the impacts of external factors on domestic interest rates and nominal exchange rates. From 1

January 2011 to 31 December 2018, I estimate a VAR model including domestic 3-months interest rates, the logarithm of the nominal exchange rate against the US Dollar, 3-months US interest rates and iShares MSCI Emerging Markets ETF. To be able to eliminate the serial correlation in the residuals, we use a specification with 3 lags. By following ([16], p. 12) "in order to identify the impulse responses, errors were orthogonalised by a Cholesky decomposition".

3.1 The full period (January 1, 2011–December 31, 2018)

VAR test reveals that for the period of 2011–2019, Turkish short-term interest rates and the USD/TRY exchange rate are not significantly affected by the US short-term interest rates in the short run. However, after our preliminary analysis, we increase the lag lengths to see if the US short-term interest rates have significant impact on Turkish interest rates and the exchange rate in longer term. The results reveal that while the exchange rate is not affected by the US short-term interest rates even in longer term; with 10 days lag interval the US short-term interest rates has a significant impact on the Turkish short-term interest rates at 90% confidence level. Therefore, for the examined period, we conclude that while the US short-term interest rates do not affect exchange rates in Turkey, Turkish short-term interest rates show a significant positive response to the shocks from the US after 10 days.

When we examine the impact of emerging markets on Turkish short-term interest rates and exchange rates we see that, emerging market risk premia has a stronger effect compared to the short-term US interest rates. According to that, the shocks coming from the emerging markets significantly affect the Turkish short-term interest rates and USD/TRY in the first 2 days. Unlike the US short-term interest rates, the impact of the emerging markets risk premia on the Turkish short-term interest rates and Turkish exchange rate disappear in the longer term.

To be able to explain the general pattern of the response of Turkish short-term interest rates and the exchange rate to the US short-term interest rates and the emerging market risk premia we perform the impulse response functions.

Figure 5 presents the impulse response functions of short-term interest rates of Turkey and USD/TRY exchange rate to the short-term interest rates of USA and the emerging market risk premia.

Figure 5 shows the impulse response functions of USD/TRY and the Turkish short-term interest rates to one percentage point US interest rate shock and emerging market risk premia shock. First, it is worth noting that the impact of the US interest rate shock to the exchange rate reaches its peak after 1 week while the impact of the US short-term interest rate shock to the Turkish short-term interest rates reaches its peak after 10 days. The interesting point is, while the US interest shocks affect Turkish exchange rate positively during the first 4 days, after the 4th day it starts to have a negative impact. However, the estimated impact on the exchange rate is not significantly different from zero during 10 days period, confirming that the exchange rate in Turkey is not affected by the US interest rates. The impact of the short-term US interest rates become significant on the short-term interest rates of Turkey on the 10th day confirming that short-term interest rates in Turkey are significantly affected by the US rates.

On the other hand, interest rate and the exchange rate react to emerging market risk premia shocks in a different way. According to that, the Turkish currency responds to emerging markets risk premia significantly and drastically on the first few days with increasing trend after the fourth day while Turkish short-term interest rate's response deepens after the fourth day and reaches its peak on the 9th day.

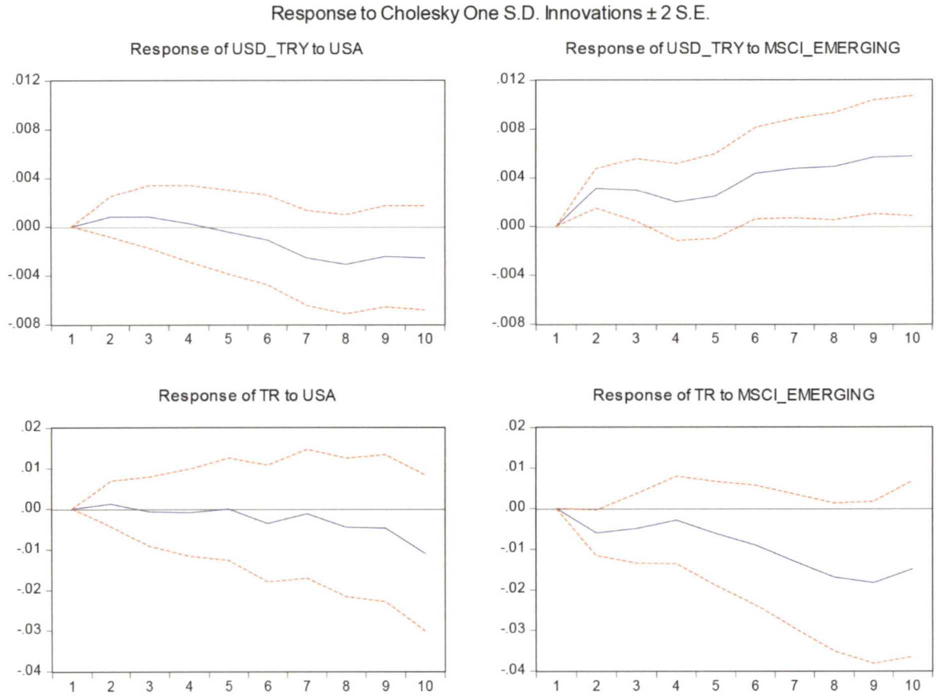

Figure 5.
Impulse response functions: innovations ± 2 standard errors. Impact on interest rates and exchange rates (logs) of percentage point shock to US interest rates and emerging markets risk.

3.2 The political stress #1 (July 29, 2011–August 11, 2011)

During the political stress #1 emerging markets risk premia significantly affects both the USD/TRY pair and the Turkish short-term interest rates. The USD/TRY pair responds significantly on the first day while short-term interest rate responds to the shocks coming from emerging markets on both the first and the second days.

During this politically stressed period, while the US short-term interest rate significantly affects the exchange rate on the second day, it has no significant impact on the short-term interest rates on neither the first nor the second day.

3.3 The political stress #2 (May 28, 2013–June 20, 2013)

Results reveal that during the political stress #2, neither the Turkish short-term interest rates nor the exchange rate in Turkey are significantly affected by both the US short-term interest rates and the emerging market risk premia. Therefore, we can clearly declare that the Gezi Park incidents cause Turkish capital markets to enter an extra sensitive period to domestic developments while external shocks stop affecting the short-term interest rates and the exchange rate. In other words, during this stressed period, the short-term interest rates and the USD/TRY pair respond to domestic shocks/news instead of external factors.

3.4 The political stress #3 (December 17, 2013–January 3, 2014)

During the politically stressed period #3, the Turkish Lira depreciates, Borsa Istanbul crashes and interest rates rise significantly. VAR analysis reveals that the reasons of these drastic moves are totally domestic. According to that, during that period, neither emerging market risk premia nor the US short-term interest rates significantly affect the short-term interest rates and the exchange rates in Turkey.

3.5 The political stress #4 (July 31, 2014–August 15, 2014)

Prior to 2014 presidential election, Turkish money markets show instability during a 10 days period. During that rather politically stressed period, Borsa Istanbul declines significantly and Turkish Lira depreciates. During this short period, VAR analysis reveals that external shocks do not have any significant impacts on the market. According to that, neither exchange rates nor interest rates respond to any shocks from the US interest rates and the emerging markets.

3.6 The political stress #5 (June 7, 2015–August 25, 2015)

The fifth political stress has the same impact with the previous stresses as during that period the external factors do not have any significant effect on the short-term interest rates and the exchange rates of Turkey. According to that, during that period, sharp depreciation of the Turkish Lira and the rise in the interest rates occur due to domestic developments.

3.7 The political stress #6 (November 24, 2015–November 29, 2015)

The results reveal different conclusion regarding the impacts of the external shocks during the politically stressed times for this specific incident. According that, during the political stress that arises due to shootdown of Russian plane on Turkish border, the Turkish currency is significantly affected by the short-term US interest rates. During that period, Turkish currency significantly responds to the changes on the US short-term interest rates in the first and the second days. During that period, the exchange rate significantly responds to also the emerging risk premia in the second day. However, Turkish short-term interest rates are not significantly affected by any of those external factors during the stress period.

3.8 The political stress #7 (July 15, 2016–July 30, 2016)

After the military coup attempt, the exchange rate in Turkey starts to show significant response to the shocks that are coming from the emerging markets. During that period emerging risk premia has a significant impact on the short-term interest rates too. Differently from the previous political stress, this time the US short-term interest rates do not have any significant impact on the exchange rate. However, this time, the Turkish short-term interest rate significantly responds to the shocks coming from the US interest rates.

3.9 The political stress #8 (July 2, 2018–October 2, 2018)

Probably, in the last decade, Turkey has experienced the deepest financial stress during this politically stress period. Right after Turkey and the USA start to have a serious diplomatic crisis due to trial of Pastor Branson, the Turkish Lira drastically depreciates and Turkish Central Bank has to increase the interest rates dramatically. During that period, our results show that the Turkish Lira and the short-term interest rates are not affected by the external shocks at all. As expected, during that period domestic news play significant role on the value of the Turkish Lira and the short-term interest rates.

3.10 Politically tranquil periods with significant depreciation of Turkish Lira and rise in interest rates

According to **Figure 4**, although we do not identify any political crisis, Turkish Lira depreciates and short-term interest rate rises significantly during the fourth quarter of 2011, the first quarter of 2017 and the fourth quarter of 2017. To be able to understand the reasons of these changes, we run analysis specifically for these periods. The results reveal that the changes on the short-term interest rates and the exchange rate occur as a respond to the shocks from emerging markets in the fourth quarter of 2011 and the fourth quarter of 2017 while the depreciation of the Turkish Lira and the increase in interest rates in the first quarter of 2017 occur as a strong respond to the shocks coming from the US short-term interest rates.

4. Conclusion

This chapter analyses the reaction of short-term interest rate and exchange rate of Turkey to the external shocks and how this reaction changes according to domestic political tension. For this purpose, the reaction of interest rates and exchange rates to the American interest rate volatility and emerging market risk factor is tested for the period of 2011–2019. During that period, we identified eight major politically stressed periods that have significant negative impact on Turkish money markets.

The primary result that we get from the VAR test for the period of 2011–2019 is that Turkish short-term interest rates and the USD/TRY exchange rate are not significantly affected by the US short-term interest rates in the short run. However, Turkish short-term interest rates significantly respond to the US short-term interest rates after 10 days. On the other hand, emerging market risk premia seems to be much more important factor on Turkish short-term interest rates and the exchange rate as during the 2011–2019 period, Turkish short-term interest rates and the exchange rate significantly respond to the shocks coming from emerging markets in the first 2 days.

If we sum up the impacts of each political stress period on the impacts of external factors on the domestic interest rates and the exchange rate, we get a blurred picture as it is difficult to generalize the impacts of political stresses. According to that, while the political stress #1 and the political stress #7 do not change how external factors affect the domestic interest rate and the exchange rate as those keep significantly responding to emerging market risk premia and the short-term US interest, during the political stresses #2, #3, #4, #5, and #8, neither exchange rates nor interest rates respond to any shocks from the US interest rates and the emerging markets. Therefore, we suggest that while the early retirement request of commanders of Turkish Army and military coup attempt did not create strong enough impact to change the pricing structure of Turkish assets and/or perception of the investors; the Gezi Park incidents, the operation of FETO terror organization to the government authorities, 2014 presidential election, 7th June 2015 general elections and afterward, and the announcement of new cabinet after 2018 elections and the Branson incident were strong enough to change the pricing priorities of investors on Turkish risky assets. Following those developments, domestic news seem to have more significant effect on the short-term interest rates and the exchange rate compared to the external factors. Only during the political stress period #6, shooting down of Russian plane, created mixed impact on the external factors as during this period the Turkish currency significantly responded to the US short-term interest rates in shorter period while it kept significantly responding to the emerging market risk premia.

The findings of this paper are quite important to understand how an emerging country can deal or should deal with a possible financial shock/crisis. According to this, the first and maybe the most important outcome of the study was that although an emerging country is in a politically stressed situation, this stress's impact on the money markets change according to the dynamics of the situation. While a fully domestic development may cause financial market to separate from the rest of the world or the countries that is normally strongly integrated with, another negative development that occurs due to foreign diplomatic issues might have an opposite impact. Therefore, policy makers should primarily determine and examine the reasons of a political tension to foresee the possible consequences in the financial markets. For the Turkish case, this study clearly showed that while during the tranquil periods Turkey is significantly integrated with both the US and the emerging markets and any shocks from those markets significantly affect both interest rates and the exchange rates, some political developments, especially army and USA related ones, cause Turkey to negatively separate from those markets. Secondly, this study quantitatively proved that the shocks that are originated from the group of emerging markets significantly affect other emerging markets in very short term while shocks from a developed country, USA in our case, show its impacts in a longer term. In this case, policy makers should be aware of the danger that instability of an emerging country may have a significant impact on their financial markets very quickly. In other words, while an emerging country has strong and healthy dynamics, a negative shock from other emerging countries may also negatively and significantly affect that specific country in the first or second day. Therefore, policy makers should be aware of the time periods while taking precautions to the negative developments in other countries.

As a result, the findings of this chapter clearly prove that an emerging country is open to financial shocks even if the country is politically tranquil due to significant effects of the group of emerging markets and the USA. In case of a political stress, on the other hand, the situation becomes more complicated as some of the political crisis cause financial markets to react negatively internal news instead of external shocks. Therefore, in emerging countries, investors and policy makers should always consider political stability of the country, dynamics of the political tension and the risk level of the group of emerging markets in the short term and the changes in the short-term interest rates of USA in the rather longer term.

Appendix

See **Tables 1–9**.

Vector autoregression estimates				
	USD_TRY	USA	TR	MSCI_EMERGING
USD_TRY(−1)	1.239555	−0.001096	−0.149446	−0.234697
	(0.02242)	(0.00351)	(0.07595)	(0.30998)
	[55.2812]	[−0.31261]	[−1.96770]	[−0.75714]
USD_TRY(−2)	−0.428334	−0.001819	0.434834	−0.279474
	(0.03463)	(0.00541)	(0.11729)	(0.47870)
	[−12.3698]	[−0.33595]	[3.70736]	[−0.58382]
USD_TRY(−3)	0.188575	0.003611	−0.244834	0.474752
	(0.02251)	(0.00352)	(0.07624)	(0.31118)
	[8.37756]	[1.02591]	[−3.21119]	[1.52566]

Vector autoregression estimates				
	USD_TRY	**USA**	**TR**	**MSCI_EMERGING**
USA(−1)	0.078956	0.973994	−0.164896	−1.484175
	(0.13915)	(0.02176)	(0.47131)	(1.92359)
	[0.56743]	[44.7690]	[−0.34987]	[−0.77157]
USA(−2)	−0.194843	0.189506	−0.492364	0.445107
	(0.19382)	(0.03031)	(0.65652)	(2.67948)
	[−1.00526]	[6.25325]	[−0.74996]	[0.16612]
USA(−3)	0.122793	−0.162329	0.641158	1.137173
	(0.13949)	(0.02181)	(0.47246)	(1.92829)
	[0.88032]	[−7.44312]	[1.35705]	[0.58973]
TR(−1)	0.018625	−0.001770	1.175840	−0.003223
	(0.00649)	(0.00101)	(0.02198)	(0.08970)
	[2.87047]	[−1.74446]	[53.5019]	[−0.03593]
TR(−2)	−0.031462	0.001251	−0.158691	0.110968
	(0.00993)	(0.00155)	(0.03362)	(0.13723)
	[−3.16940]	[0.80626]	[−4.71967]	[0.80864]
TR(−3)	0.011875	0.000448	−0.022727	−0.112278
	(0.00647)	(0.00101)	(0.02191)	(0.08941)
	[1.83610]	[0.44281]	[−1.03744]	[−1.25577]
MSCI_EMERGING(−1)	0.006609	−0.000374	−0.013413	0.950738
	(0.00164)	(0.00026)	(0.00556)	(0.02268)
	[4.02779]	[−1.45922]	[−2.41343]	[41.9154]
MSCI_EMERGING(−2)	−0.008802	6.42E-05	0.019646	0.033825
	(0.00229)	(0.00036)	(0.00776)	(0.03166)
	[−3.84306]	[0.17935]	[2.53237]	[1.06829]
MSCI_EMERGING(−3)	0.002344	0.000305	−0.004392	0.004523
	(0.00165)	(0.00026)	(0.00558)	(0.02277)
	[1.42275]	[1.18279]	[−0.78721]	[0.19864]
C	0.001672	−0.000695	−0.104660	0.530523
	(0.01176)	(0.00184)	(0.03982)	(0.16252)
	[0.14220]	[−0.37831]	[−2.62837]	[3.26443]
R-squared	0.998765	0.999927	0.999116	0.985729
Adj. R-squared	0.998758	0.999926	0.999111	0.985646
Sum sq. resids	2.957368	0.072297	33.92978	565.1823
S.E. equation	0.037798	0.005910	0.128028	0.522527
F-statistic	139543.2	2,358,791.	194978.8	11914.92
Log likelihood	3873.742	7739.029	1332.489	−1597.100
Akaike AIC	−3.706906	−7.418175	−1.266912	1.545943
Schwarz SC	−3.671697	−7.382966	−1.231703	1.581152
Mean dependent	2.728274	0.738451	11.06632	40.88733
SD dependent	1.072606	0.689107	4.293795	4.361402

Sample (adjusted): 1/06/2011–12/31/2018.
Included observations: 2083 after adjustments.
Standard errors in () & t-statistics in [].

Table 1.
VAR estimates result for full period.

Vector autoregression estimates				
	USD_TRY	**TR**	**USA**	**MSCI_EMERGING**
USD_TRY(−1)	−0.872545	8.859426	−0.060340	−31.14791
	(0.62071)	(3.47853)	(0.29360)	(41.8594)
	[−1.40573]	[2.54689]	[−0.20552]	[−0.74411]
USD_TRY(−2)	0.308087	13.98951	0.103715	−92.17556
	(0.60804)	(3.40756)	(0.28761)	(41.0055)
	[0.50668]	[4.10543]	[0.36061]	[−2.24788]
TR(−1)	−0.021083	0.888519	−0.005818	−4.368654
	(0.04691)	(0.26291)	(0.02219)	(3.16377)
	[−0.44939]	[3.37956]	[−0.26218]	[−1.38084]
TR(−2)	0.127874	−0.081052	−0.029449	−12.88844
	(0.05263)	(0.29492)	(0.02489)	(3.54897)
	[2.42989]	[−0.27483]	[−1.18308]	[−3.63160]
USA(−1)	1.360505	2.451433	0.474769	−46.93249
	(1.13015)	(6.33354)	(0.53457)	(76.2157)
	[1.20382]	[0.38706]	[0.88814]	[−0.61579]
USA(−2)	1.357323	−27.54796	0.247523	32.81856
	(1.41483)	(7.92892)	(0.66922)	(95.4140)
	[0.95935]	[−3.47437]	[0.36987]	[0.34396]
MSCI_EMERGING(−1)	−0.013139	0.090067	−0.001294	0.300612
	(0.00716)	(0.04014)	(0.00339)	(0.48306)
	[−1.83430]	[2.24372]	[−0.38187]	[0.62231]
MSCI_EMERGING(−2)	−0.002236	0.142830	0.002761	0.051437
	(0.00847)	(0.04748)	(0.00401)	(0.57139)
	[−0.26393]	[3.00808]	[0.68888]	[0.09002]
C	1.753591	−41.44923	0.239769	391.0476
	(2.30845)	(12.9369)	(1.09191)	(155.678)
	[0.75964]	[−3.20396]	[0.21959]	[2.51190]
R-squared	0.981377	0.991826	0.951979	0.986179
Adj. R-squared	0.906885	0.959132	0.759893	0.930895
Sum sq. resids	0.000261	0.008212	5.85E-05	1.189129
S.E. equation	0.011434	0.064077	0.005408	0.771080
F-statistic	13.17424	30.33649	4.956014	17.83851
Log likelihood	42.95073	23.99218	51.18588	−3.372616
Akaike AIC	−6.172859	−2.725851	−7.670159	2.249567
Schwarz SC	−5.847309	−2.400300	−7.344609	2.575117
Mean dependent	1.741182	8.368442	0.272727	42.97664
SD dependent	0.037470	0.316965	0.011037	2.933228

Sample: 7/29/2011–8/12/2011.
Included observations: 11.
Standard errors in () & t-statistics in [].

Table 2.
VAR estimates result for political stress #1.

Vector autoregression estimates				
	USD_TRY	TR	USA	MSCI_EMERGING
USD_TRY(−1)	1.045822	1.551895	0.082439	−16.61406
	(0.35577)	(3.63916)	(0.07309)	(17.9657)
	[2.93957]	[0.42644]	[1.12787]	[−0.92477]
USD_TRY(−2)	−0.592774	0.541974	0.086876	4.068066
	(0.38266)	(3.91418)	(0.07862)	(19.3234)
	[−1.54909]	[0.13846]	[1.10506]	[0.21053]
TR(−1)	0.000282	0.879367	−0.015476	1.021491
	(0.03042)	(0.31120)	(0.00625)	(1.53631)
	[0.00926]	[2.82575]	[−2.47605]	[0.66490]
TR(−2)	0.020745	−0.085642	0.007593	−1.961514
	(0.02836)	(0.29005)	(0.00583)	(1.43189)
	[0.73162]	[−0.29527]	[1.30335]	[−1.36988]
USA(−1)	1.896724	18.28130	−0.244931	−19.59458
	(1.23033)	(12.5849)	(0.25277)	(62.1287)
	[1.54164]	[1.45264]	[−0.96899]	[−0.31539]
USA(−2)	−0.351707	15.14300	0.055503	−52.90086
	(1.28545)	(13.1487)	(0.26409)	(64.9120)
	[−0.27361]	[1.15167]	[0.21017]	[−0.81496]
MSCI_EMERGING(−1)	−0.006059	−0.069716	0.002865	0.531484
	(0.00809)	(0.08272)	(0.00166)	(0.40836)
	[−0.74921]	[−0.84281]	[1.72434]	[1.30151]
MSCI_EMERGING(−2)	0.011379	−0.007283	−0.003909	−0.024268
	(0.00942)	(0.09636)	(0.00194)	(0.47571)
	[1.20785]	[−0.07558]	[−2.01978]	[−0.05101]
C	0.270639	−8.592797	0.095488	68.32132
	(0.88691)	(9.07206)	(0.18221)	(44.7866)
	[0.30515]	[−0.94717]	[0.52404]	[1.52549]
R-squared	0.779097	0.964512	0.648236	0.870906
Adj. R-squared	0.602375	0.936121	0.366825	0.767630
Sum sq. resids	0.002105	0.220288	8.89E-05	5.368774
S.E. equation	0.014510	0.148421	0.002981	0.732719
F-statistic	4.408603	33.97284	2.303518	8.432841
Log likelihood	59.56320	15.38413	89.63188	−14.95336
Akaike AIC	−5.322442	−0.672013	−8.487566	2.521406
Schwarz SC	−4.875076	−0.224648	−8.040200	2.968772
Mean dependent	1.884921	5.980695	0.271579	40.16632
SD dependent	0.023011	0.587241	0.003746	1.520014

Sample: 5/28/2013–6/21/2013.
Included observations: 19.
Standard errors in () & t-statistics in [].

Table 3.
VAR estimates result for political stress #2.

DOI: http://dx.doi.org/10.5772/intechopen.89931

Vector autoregression estimates				
	USD_TRY	**TR**	**USA**	**MSCI_EMERGING**
USD_TRY(−1)	0.252091	4.905135	−0.100362	−3.579565
	(1.02806)	(3.21845)	(0.17927)	(6.53266)
	[0.24521]	[1.52407]	[−0.55983]	[−0.54795]
USD_TRY(−2)	−0.294757	8.237847	0.007630	20.28858
	(1.42700)	(4.46736)	(0.24884)	(9.06764)
	[−0.20656]	[1.84401]	[0.03066]	[2.23747]
TR(−1)	0.108817	−0.159976	0.025424	1.179018
	(0.15216)	(0.47636)	(0.02653)	(0.96690)
	[0.71513]	[−0.33583]	[0.95816]	[1.21938]
TR(−2)	0.043346	−0.073717	0.004355	0.396928
	(0.06720)	(0.21036)	(0.01172)	(0.42699)
	[0.64507]	[−0.35042]	[0.37162]	[0.92960]
USA(−1)	4.359186	6.880054	1.223262	−8.315462
	(5.69159)	(17.8181)	(0.99249)	(36.1663)
	[0.76590]	[0.38613]	[1.23251]	[−0.22992]
USA(−2)	−4.603798	−12.52887	−1.557584	−176.5719
	(10.1715)	(31.8428)	(1.77369)	(64.6331)
	[−0.45262]	[−0.39346]	[−0.87816]	[−2.73191]
MSCI_EMERGING(−1)	−0.042445	−0.279831	−0.012791	−1.229423
	(0.07507)	(0.23500)	(0.01309)	(0.47700)
	[−0.56543]	[−1.19075]	[−0.97716]	[−2.57741]
MSCI_EMERGING(−2)	0.076973	0.263341	0.010266	0.595434
	(0.06557)	(0.20527)	(0.01143)	(0.41664)
	[1.17394]	[1.28292]	[0.89786]	[1.42913]
C	−0.504984	−14.32025	0.366730	64.21933
	(2.80039)	(8.76691)	(0.48833)	(17.7947)
	[−0.18033]	[−1.63344]	[0.75099]	[3.60891]
R-squared	0.944309	0.994128	0.799905	0.977004
Adj. R-squared	0.498785	0.947151	−0.800856	0.793032
Sum sq. resids	0.000592	0.005804	1.80E−05	0.023913
S.E. equation	0.024336	0.076186	0.004244	0.154638
F-statistic	2.119544	21.16193	0.499703	5.310618
Log likelihood	34.48162	23.06937	51.94686	15.99023
Akaike AIC	−5.096325	−2.813875	−8.589371	−1.398046
Schwarz SC	−4.823998	−2.541548	−8.317045	−1.125720
Mean dependent	2.093070	8.858114	0.249000	40.94500
SD dependent	0.034374	0.331400	0.003162	0.339910

Sample: 12/17/2013–12/30/2013.
Included observations: 10.
Standard errors in () & t-statistics in [].

Table 4.
VAR estimates result for political stress #3.

Vector autoregression estimates				
	USD_TRY	TR	USA	MSCI_EMERGING
USD_TRY(−1)	−0.519237	5.242203	−0.018683	12.66113
	(0.53772)	(8.59526)	(0.07212)	(28.5601)
	[−0.96563]	[0.60989]	[−0.25906]	[0.44332]
USD_TRY(−2)	−0.521707	3.284314	−0.116449	34.40483
	(0.38776)	(6.19818)	(0.05201)	(20.5951)
	[−1.34546]	[0.52988]	[−2.23911]	[1.67053]
TR(−1)	0.033199	0.584900	−0.002042	−1.450924
	(0.02810)	(0.44925)	(0.00377)	(1.49274)
	[1.18128]	[1.30196]	[−0.54171]	[−0.97198]
TR(−2)	0.024623	0.209647	−0.007635	0.635585
	(0.03095)	(0.49468)	(0.00415)	(1.64371)
	[0.79564]	[0.42380]	[−1.83935]	[0.38668]
USA(−1)	−2.852733	−1.444260	−0.348541	65.70581
	(2.87562)	(45.9662)	(0.38569)	(152.735)
	[−0.99204]	[−0.03142]	[−0.90369]	[0.43019]
USA(−2)	1.643630	56.99025	−0.609977	39.20152
	(2.56418)	(40.9878)	(0.34391)	(136.193)
	[0.64100]	[1.39042]	[−1.77363]	[0.28784]
MSCI_EMERGING(−1)	−0.009292	0.051124	−0.001046	1.098503
	(0.01213)	(0.19387)	(0.00163)	(0.64419)
	[−0.76609]	[0.26370]	[−0.64291]	[1.70524]
MSCI_EMERGING(−2)	0.012677	−0.037399	−0.002046	−0.335273
	(0.01016)	(0.16248)	(0.00136)	(0.53989)
	[1.24711]	[−0.23017]	[−1.50076]	[−0.62100]
C	3.995803	−30.06631	0.974848	−107.8384
	(2.68089)	(42.8534)	(0.35957)	(142.392)
	[1.49048]	[−0.70161]	[2.71117]	[−0.75733]
R-squared	0.893257	0.940998	0.955591	0.778050
Adj. R-squared	0.608608	0.783658	0.837167	0.186182
Sum sq. resids	0.000172	0.043909	3.09E−06	0.484785
S.E. equation	0.007568	0.120980	0.001015	0.401989
F-statistic	3.138103	5.980680	8.069210	1.314567
Log likelihood	49.89570	16.63606	74.00372	2.226473
Akaike AIC	−6.815950	−1.272677	−10.83395	1.128921
Schwarz SC	−6.452270	−0.908997	−10.47027	1.492601
Mean dependent	2.151733	9.187219	0.234792	44.07875
SD dependent	0.012098	0.260102	0.002516	0.445605

Sample: 7/31/2014–8/15/2014.
Included observations: 12.
Standard errors in () & t-statistics in [].

Table 5.
VAR estimates result for political stress #4.

Vector autoregression estimates				
	USD_TRY	**TR**	**USA**	**MSCI_EMERGING**
USD_TRY(−1)	0.708805	0.249663	0.034715	2.442156
	(0.16209)	(0.45042)	(0.02559)	(3.85036)
	[4.37278]	[0.55429]	[1.35656]	[0.63427]
USD_TRY(−2)	0.122357	0.043897	−0.025023	1.655415
	(0.16238)	(0.45120)	(0.02564)	(3.85707)
	[0.75354]	[0.09729]	[−0.97614]	[0.42919]
TR(−1)	−0.004405	0.903572	−0.009074	−2.033973
	(0.05723)	(0.15902)	(0.00903)	(1.35938)
	[−0.07697]	[5.68205]	[−1.00429]	[−1.49625]
TR(−2)	−0.064607	−0.116529	−0.001492	0.684540
	(0.05883)	(0.16348)	(0.00929)	(1.39745)
	[−1.09819]	[−0.71282]	[−0.16062]	[0.48985]
USA(−1)	0.329242	1.942183	0.669188	−15.31464
	(1.00376)	(2.78919)	(0.15847)	(23.8431)
	[0.32801]	[0.69633]	[4.22288]	[−0.64231]
USA(−2)	0.969726	0.107627	0.224866	−24.57049
	(1.01086)	(2.80893)	(0.15959)	(24.0118)
	[0.95930]	[0.03832]	[1.40904]	[−1.02327]
MSCI_EMERGING(−1)	−0.009986	−0.010206	0.000254	0.938702
	(0.00657)	(0.01826)	(0.00104)	(0.15607)
	[−1.51989]	[−0.55900]	[0.24527]	[6.01475]
MSCI_EMERGING(−2)	0.009639	0.019322	−0.001503	−0.141877
	(0.00673)	(0.01869)	(0.00106)	(0.15978)
	[1.43299]	[1.03376]	[−1.41540]	[−0.88797]
C	0.880645	0.680372	0.173718	23.55633
	(0.46135)	(1.28196)	(0.07283)	(10.9587)
	[1.90886]	[0.53073]	[2.38512]	[2.14956]
R-squared	0.945737	0.897486	0.968769	0.962453
Adj. R-squared	0.936693	0.880401	0.963564	0.956195
Sum sq. resids	0.019811	0.152969	0.000494	11.17816
S.E. equation	0.020316	0.056452	0.003207	0.482575
F-statistic	104.5732	52.52882	186.1174	153.7995
Log likelihood	146.1108	87.85686	251.3305	−34.45046
Akaike AIC	−4.810905	−2.766907	−8.502823	1.524577
Schwarz SC	−4.488318	−2.444320	−8.180236	1.847164
Mean dependent	2.743363	11.41014	0.297242	37.78491
SD dependent	0.080744	0.163236	0.016803	2.305703

Sample: 6/08/2015 8/25/2015.
Included observations: 57.
Standard errors in () & t-statistics in [].

Table 6.
VAR estimates result for political stress #5.

Vector autoregression estimates				
	USD_TRY	TR	USA	MSCI_EMERGING
USD_TRY(−1)	0.208853	0.554838	−0.258267	−7.360014
	(0.21444)	(0.27058)	(0.20349)	(13.1649)
	[0.97393]	[2.05054]	[−1.26918]	[−0.55906]
USD_TRY(−2)	0.028340	−0.576283	0.151205	−10.63891
	(0.26409)	(0.33322)	(0.25060)	(16.2126)
	[0.10731]	[−1.72944]	[0.60337]	[−0.65621]
TR(−1)	−0.847586	0.133623	−0.028234	−17.66526
	(0.41552)	(0.52430)	(0.39430)	(25.5093)
	[−2.03980]	[0.25486]	[−0.07161]	[−0.69250]
TR(−2)	−0.471574	−0.045990	0.110749	−0.187963
	(0.36342)	(0.45856)	(0.34486)	(22.3107)
	[−1.29759]	[−0.10029]	[0.32114]	[−0.00842]
USA(−1)	−2.406126	−0.632717	1.249959	−80.84426
	(1.16439)	(1.46920)	(1.10491)	(71.4826)
	[−2.06643]	[−0.43065]	[1.13127]	[−1.13096]
USA(−2)	3.931361	0.807797	−0.060307	66.93084
	(1.29648)	(1.63587)	(1.23026)	(79.5917)
	[3.03234]	[0.49380]	[−0.04902]	[0.84093]
MSCI_EMERGING(−1)	0.010020	−0.008902	0.004755	−0.659546
	(0.01389)	(0.01753)	(0.01318)	(0.85275)
	[0.72132]	[−0.50792]	[0.36075]	[−0.77344]
MSCI_EMERGING(−2)	0.035343	−0.011427	0.000584	0.064169
	(0.01135)	(0.01432)	(0.01077)	(0.69677)
	[3.11402]	[−0.79790]	[0.05422]	[0.09210]
C	15.00712	11.04252	−0.880388	315.4749
	(5.87354)	(7.41108)	(5.57353)	(360.580)
	[2.55504]	[1.49000]	[−0.15796]	[0.87491]
R-squared	0.976238	0.940271	0.993659	0.937157
Adj. R-squared	0.881190	0.701355	0.968296	0.685786
Sum sq. resids	6.20E−05	9.86E−05	5.58E−05	0.233487
S.E. equation	0.005566	0.007023	0.005281	0.341677
F-statistic	10.27098	3.935577	39.17780	3.728184
Log likelihood	50.87040	48.31268	51.44711	5.580570
Akaike AIC	−7.612800	−7.147761	−7.717657	0.621715
Schwarz SC	−7.287250	−6.822210	−7.392107	0.947265
Mean dependent	2.900682	11.35010	0.435164	34.01700
SD dependent	0.016147	0.012850	0.029661	0.609542

Sample: 11/24/2015–12/08/2015.
Included observations: 11.
Standard errors in () & t-statistics in [].

Table 7.
VAR estimates result for political stress #6.

Vector autoregression estimates				
	USD_TRY	**TR**	**USA**	**MSCI_EMERGING**
USD_TRY(−1)	−0.037991	1.379474	0.026738	1.548057
	(0.15992)	(0.37246)	(0.03780)	(1.29406)
	[−0.23756]	[3.70373]	[0.70742]	[1.19628]
USD_TRY(−2)	0.664323	0.991110	−0.007986	−2.964535
	(0.21112)	(0.49171)	(0.04990)	(1.70841)
	[3.14659]	[2.01564]	[−0.16005]	[−1.73526]
TR(−1)	−0.162109	0.281267	0.021652	1.083173
	(0.09284)	(0.21622)	(0.02194)	(0.75124)
	[−1.74614]	[1.30083]	[0.98678]	[1.44184]
TR(−2)	−0.048103	0.104220	−0.013276	−0.898872
	(0.07228)	(0.16834)	(0.01708)	(0.58489)
	[−0.66551]	[0.61910]	[−0.77712]	[−1.53684]
USA(−1)	2.328077	−12.13171	1.062720	14.50641
	(1.90754)	(4.44268)	(0.45085)	(15.4357)
	[1.22046]	[−2.73072]	[2.35717]	[0.93980]
USA(−2)	−2.262053	13.16730	0.004139	−7.328605
	(1.82020)	(4.23925)	(0.43020)	(14.7289)
	[−1.24275]	[3.10604]	[0.00962]	[−0.49757]
MSCI_EMERGING(−1)	−0.116796	0.068353	−0.010143	−0.187650
	(0.04461)	(0.10390)	(0.01054)	(0.36098)
	[−2.61818]	[0.65790]	[−0.96199]	[−0.51984]
MSCI_EMERGING(−2)	0.023493	−0.263795	−0.004722	−0.082381
	(0.03527)	(0.08215)	(0.00834)	(0.28544)
	[0.66601]	[−3.21096]	[−0.56636]	[−0.28861]
C	6.501998	5.274677	0.351928	42.78517
	(2.04631)	(4.76587)	(0.48364)	(16.5586)
	[3.17743]	[1.10676]	[0.72766]	[2.58386]
R-squared	0.855084	0.959389	0.991451	0.725483
Adj. R-squared	0.661862	0.905240	0.980052	0.359461
Sum sq. resids	0.002215	0.012015	0.000124	0.145044
S.E. equation	0.019214	0.044750	0.004541	0.155480
F-statistic	4.425407	17.71779	86.97880	1.982072
Log likelihood	44.86974	32.18810	66.50640	13.50670
Akaike AIC	−4.782632	−3.091747	−7.667519	−0.600893
Schwarz SC	−4.357802	−2.666916	−7.242689	−0.176063
Mean dependent	3.025113	9.883607	0.729647	35.91900
SD dependent	0.033043	0.145372	0.032153	0.194268

Sample: 7/15/2016–8/04/2016.
Included observations: 15.
Standard errors in () & t-statistics in [].

Table 8.
VAR estimates result for political stress #7.

Vector autoregression estimates				
	USD_TRY	TR	USA	MSCI_EMERGING
USD_TRY(−1)	1.112781	−0.296064	−0.009584	−0.251992
	(0.14951)	(0.30256)	(0.00484)	(0.38034)
	[7.44288]	[−0.97852]	[−1.97877]	[−0.66254]
USD_TRY(−2)	−0.203608	0.660003	0.004431	−0.652522
	(0.14567)	(0.29479)	(0.00472)	(0.37057)
	[−1.39776]	[2.23891]	[0.93908]	[−1.76088]
TR(−1)	0.129738	1.050609	0.000190	−0.234949
	(0.06417)	(0.12986)	(0.00208)	(0.16324)
	[2.02184]	[8.09048]	[0.09140]	[−1.43930]
TR(−2)	−0.100454	−0.143475	0.002212	0.448261
	(0.06676)	(0.13511)	(0.00216)	(0.16984)
	[−1.50463]	[−1.06192]	[1.02261]	[2.63932]
USA(−1)	−3.823444	−4.286335	0.804341	−9.608025
	(4.55697)	(9.22198)	(0.14762)	(11.5926)
	[−0.83903]	[−0.46480]	[5.44863]	[−0.82881]
USA(−2)	1.561428	12.25069	0.093564	−4.784711
	(4.43729)	(8.97979)	(0.14375)	(11.2881)
	[0.35189]	[1.36425]	[0.65090]	[−0.42387]
MSCI_EMERGING(−1)	0.085443	0.064802	−0.000532	0.614351
	(0.05032)	(0.10183)	(0.00163)	(0.12800)
	[1.49812]	[0.63640]	[−0.32661]	[4.79958]
MSCI_EMERGING(−2)	−0.021460	−0.075181	0.001042	0.162597
	(0.05144)	(0.10409)	(0.00167)	(0.13085)
	[−0.41721]	[−0.72225]	[0.62550]	[1.24262]
C	2.387621	−18.00681	0.193460	43.62729
	(4.73605)	(9.58438)	(0.15342)	(12.0481)
	[0.50414]	[−1.87877]	[1.26095]	[3.62108]
R-squared	0.954022	0.986646	0.949950	0.831893
Adj. R-squared	0.947681	0.984804	0.943046	0.808706
Sum sq. resids	1.615137	6.614623	0.001695	10.45240
S.E. equation	0.166875	0.337706	0.005406	0.424516
F-statistic	150.4354	535.6535	137.6044	35.87724
Log likelihood	29.72776	−17.50265	259.5212	−32.83053
Akaike AIC	−0.618739	0.791124	−7.478245	1.248673
Schwarz SC	−0.322587	1.087277	−7.182093	1.544825
Mean dependent	5.668028	22.54157	2.338678	43.14940
SD dependent	0.729557	2.739510	0.022652	0.970606

Sample: 7/02/2018–10/02/2018.
Included observations: 67.
Standard errors in () & t-statistics in [].

Table 9.
VAR estimates result for political stress #8.

Author details

Dogus Emin
Social Sciences University of Ankara, Turkey

*Address all correspondence to: dogus.emin@asbu.edu.tr

References

[1] Longstaff FA. The sub-prime credit crisis and contagion in financial markets. Journal of Financial Economics. 2010;**97**:436-450

[2] Reinhart CM, Rogoff KS. The aftermath of the financial crisis. In: Working Paper. National Bureau of Economic Research; 2009

[3] Brunnermeier MK, Pedersen LH. Market liquidity and funding liquidity. Review of Financial Studies. 2009;**22**: 2201-2238

[4] Melvin M, Taylor PM. The crisis in the foreign exchange market. Journal of International Money and Finance. 2009; **28**:1317-1330

[5] Tang DY, Yan H. Market conditions, default risk and credit spread. Journal of Banking & Finance. 2010;**34**:743-753

[6] Billio M, Gatemansky M, Lo AW, Pelizzon L. Measuring Systemic Risk in the Finance and Insurance Sectors. Working Paper: Massachusetts Institute of Technology; 2010

[7] Diamond WD, Rajan RG. Liquidity shortages and banking crises. Journal of Finance. 2005;**60**:615-647

[8] Enenajor E, Sebastian A, Witmer J. An assessment of the bank of Canada's term PRA facility. North American Journal of Economics and Finance. 2012; **23**:123-143

[9] McAndrews J, Sarkar A, Wang Z. The Effect of the Term Auction Facility on the London Inter-Bank Offered Rate. Federal Reserve Bank of New York; 2009 Staff Report No. 335

[10] Pais A, Stork PA. Contagion risk in the Australian banking and property sectors. Journal of Banking & Finance. 2011;**35**:681-697

[11] Sarkar A. Liquidity risk, credit risk, and the Federal Reserve's responses to the crisis. Financial Market Portfolio Management. 2009;**23**:335-348

[12] Yang HF, Liu CL, Chou YR. Interest rate risk propagation: Evidence from the credit crunch. North American Journal of Economics & Finance. 2014;**28**: 242-264

[13] Changa CL, McAleerc M, Tansuchat R. Conditional correlations and volatility spillovers between crude oil and stock index returns. North American Journal of Economics and Finance. 2013;**25**:116-138

[14] Forbes KJ, Rigobon R. No contagion, only interdependence: Measuring stock market co-movements. Journal of Finance. 2002;**57**:2223-2261

[15] Mandilaras A, Bird G. Foreign exchange markets in South-East Asia 1990–2004: An empirical analysis of spillovers during crisis and non-crisis periods. North American Journal of Economics and Finance. 2007;**18**:41-57

[16] Habib MM. Financial contagion, interest rates and the role of the exchange rate as shock absorber in Central and Eastern Europe. In: Discussion Paper. Bank of Finland Institute for Economies in Transition; 2002

[17] Edwards S. Interest rate volatility, contagion and convergence: An empirical investigation of the cases of Argentina, Chile and Mexico. Journal of Applied Economics. 1998;**1**:55-86

[18] Bernanke BS. On the predictive power of the interest rate spread. New England Economic Review. 1990; **November–December**:51-68

[19] Friedman BM, Kuttner KN. Money, income, price, and interest rates. American Economic Review. 1993;**82**: 472-492

[20] Gertler M, Hubbard RG, Kashyap A. Interest rate spread, credit constraints, and investment fluctuations: An empirical investigation. In: Hubbard RG, editor. Financial Markets and Financial Crises. Chicago: University of Chicago Press; 1991. pp. 11-31

[21] Borensztein E, Zettelmeyer J, Philippon T. Monetary Independence in Emerging Markets: Does the Exchange Rate Regime Make a Difference? Working Paper: IMF; 2001

[22] Demirel UD. The transmission of foreign interest rate shocks to a small-open economy: The role of external debt and financial integration. The B.E. Journal of Macroeconomics. 2009;**9**(1): 1-37

[23] Allegret JP, Couharde C, Guillaumin C. The impact of external shocks in East Asia: Lessons from a structural VAR model with block exogeneity. International Economics. 2012;**132**(4):35-89

[24] Andrle M, Garcia-Saltos R, Ho G. The role of domestic and external shocks in Poland: Results from an agnostic estimation procedure. In: IMF Working Paper. 2013

[25] Pelipas I, Shymanovich G, Kirchner R. International linkages and external shocks: A Global VAR Perspective for Belarus. Evidence from Different Model Specifications. Belarus: German Economic Team; 2016. Policy Study Series No. 02/2016

[26] Edwards S. Interest rates, contagion and capital controls. In: NBER Working Paper. 2000

[27] Zivot E, Wang J. Modelling Financial Time Series with S-PLUS. New York: Springer-Verlag; 2006